The Playbook

The Playbook

*A Conservative's Guide
to Becoming a Liberal Elite*

Charlie Mike Adkins

The Playbook

Copyright © 2021 Blacksmith Publishing

ISBN 978-1-956904-01-7

LCCN

Printed in the United States of America

Published by Blacksmith LLC
Fayetteville, North Carolina

www.BlacksmithPublishing.com

Direct inquiries and/or orders to the above web address.

Contents

Preface ix

Introduction 1

Chapter

1 – Understanding the Brilliance of Liberalism 3

2 – Tools of the Trade 10

3 – Racism and Other Useful Discriminatory Practices ... 22

4 – Hypocrisy 38

5 – Hate 47

6 – Outrage and the Victim Mentality 54

7 – Smug Intellectualism 63

8 – Embrace Islam 67

9 – LGBT 69

10 – Be Anti-Gun 72

11 – Violence 79

12 – Misdirection and Outright Lies 84

13 – Playing the Long Game 90

About the Author 95

Preface

My children have told me that I'm fluent in sarcasm. My buddies have told me the same thing. The genesis of this book was general conversation with family and friends, using that sarcasm to talk trash about the American political landscape. Someone would say something about a Democratic stance and act as if they supported it. Then, everyone else would jump on board in a whole sarcastic exchange. It went something like this:

Me, as move my AR-15 (that I built) to the table at my personal shooting range: "Oh yeah, I definitely don't think Americans are responsible enough to own weapons of war!"

My cousin, as he unpacks his AR-15 (that I built), safely ensures it's clear, checks the optic and puts it on the table: "You're right, especially those AR-15's. They've been known to climb out of the gun safe and just run down the street randomly killing people.

Me: "OK, let's be fair, they don't run down the street randomly killing people. They run down the street randomly killing children."

My friend, joining the conversation, bringing his AR-15 (that I built) and setting it next to the other two: "As a matter of fact, I don't think Americans should have any guns at all. All we have to do is ban guns and then all the violent crime will stop."

Me, as I unpack my suppressor from my range bag: "That's a great point, and we definitely need to make silencers illegal as well, because all the crazy conservative gun nuts just run around killing everybody silently...with their 30 caliber clip Ghost Guns."

My cousin: "On Full Semi-Auto..."
And it goes on like this for a few minutes until someone starts laughing or gets serious. "The bad thing is, the loonies really think like that. Someone should write a book..."

This led me to the initial version of "The Playbook". I began writing it in 2018, with the intent of pointing out the direction that I saw the Liberals/Socialist Democrats going, and making specific predictions about the tactics and techniques that I thought they would be using in the future. When I began writing, one of the first questions that came up was whether I would write it under my own name or use a pen name. My initial inclination was to use a pen name. I'm writing a book on how to "become" a liberal elite. I thought it would be hilarious if the author was a half-black, half Puerto Rican dude who identified as a woman. That's when Shaniqua Pelosi-Mendez was created. I bounced around the idea for a while.

Of course, my typical sarcasm came out whenever we joked about the backblast from the book: "If you don't like my book, it's just because you're a racist transphobic sexist!" Obviously, I decided not to use Shaniqua (although I'm sure she's lovely). At the time, I decided that I would just write the book and make that decision later.

The problem was that I wasn't really writing with any specific timeline for when I wanted to finish the book. I was just writing it because it was therapeutic to me to get the words out of my head and see them on the computer screen in front of me. However, this slow approach created a problem, because the Liberals were moving much faster than I anticipated. For example, in the first draft, I said that in the future, Liberals would be able to actively discriminate against whites specifically for their race, but it wouldn't be considered racist, you know, because only whites can be racist. Well, before I finished the book, that specific tactic became commonplace. Overall, the book just felt like it was already outdated, before it was even finished. So, I just stopped writing it. I shelved it and walked away. The American author Phillip Roth once said, "You can't write good satirical fiction in America because reality will quickly outdo anything you invent." This was what I felt like.

However, before I stopped writing the book, I had mentioned to a few friends that I was writing it. Fast forward a couple of years. I was visiting one of my oldest friends from my days in Special Forces. He had been the Special Forces Medical Sergeant on my ODA (Operational Detachment-Alpha, or A-Team) on my first combat deployment to Afghanistan (he's now a doctor). He and his wife knew that I had been writing the book. His wife asked me "So, where are you on your book."

I explained that I had decided against writing it and how I had come to that decision. They asked to hear some excerpts from the book. I had my computer with me, so I pulled out my computer, fired it up and scrolled through my files to the book.

As I skipped down to the middle of one of the chapters, my buddy walked back from the kitchen, where he had made us both a drink called a Moscow Mule. He handed me the copper mug and I tested it. "That's good, how do you make it?"

His wife, who had been waiting patiently, interrupted "Oh, no! No more stalling, let's hear the book!" I set the mug down and threw up my hands in mock surrender. "Ok, ok, let's see. This is from Chapter..."

I read several excerpts from the book, from two or three different chapters. I actually felt self-conscious reading it aloud to other people. In retrospect, it was somewhat odd to feel that way, because I had written it with the mindset that I would publish it. However, here I was, reading it out loud to someone else for the first time and I wasn't sure what they would think, or if others would even want to hear the ideas that I had written down. Keep in mind that I don't have a problem with public speaking. I've been an instructor of numerous subjects over the years. I've stood in front of classrooms as small as 3 people and as large as several hundred, but this was different. These were my words, my observations and my ideas. I wasn't just teaching a class from a lesson plan. This was different.

My buddy's wife just stared at me for a second and then said "Oh my gosh, you HAVE to print this! This is exactly what people need to hear right now!"

I felt like the information was dated, old, even irrelevant at this point. The country was so inundated with the election, scandals, riots, COVID-19, an erratic economy, and a never-ending news cycle, that I felt like everyone could already see the ridiculously destructive and overt actions of the left. I felt like my book was just stating the obvious and there was no need to put that out there. If I was going to do this, my book would need a facelift before it was even printed for the first time. So that's what happened. I went back to page 1 and I started over.

This book is what came from that effort. I hope that this helps expose the destructive nature of the actions being taken in this country right now. When I was deciding on a format for the book, it was obvious to me that I should try to keep the book reasonably short. I

was not trying to present an actual textbook. The book is meant to be very snarky. It is meant to be surprising, and it is intentionally tongue in cheek. It will offend some people who read it.
I'm ok with that.

tongue-in-cheek
noun, adjective / ˈtʌŋ·ɪn ˈtʃík /

1. intended to be understood as a joke, although often seeming serious:
He made some tongue-in-cheek comment about being very busy cleaning his house.

Introduction

First of all, let me say congratulations on your decision to leave conservatism behind and embrace liberalism. Now, let's complete your journey, your transition, your transformation! You must understand that just being a liberal is not enough. This is merely a steppingstone on the path towards the bigger picture. This is a small piece of the road towards a progressive Socialist society. However, that doesn't mean that we will stop there. Most Americans are oblivious of the country's slow march towards Communism. They are too busy staring at their phones and televisions to even realize that there is war raging for the future of their country.

Because of this, they are losing a war that they don't even know they are in. This is your chance to be on the winning side of that war. In the pending battles ahead, your insight into conservatives, Republicans and every other poisonous right-wing ideal will prove invaluable.

For over 240 years, the conservatives of the United States have had free reign to force their ridiculous ideology on the people of the country unchecked. They believe that "freedom" is a good thing, and they can't seem to grasp the simple idea that big government is the answer to many everyday problems.

They act like the Bill of Rights should be used by the people as a shield, as armor to protect them. However, we know the truth. We know that the Bill of Rights, in fact much of the U.S. Constitution, is merely a roadblock to our goals. Luckily, there are ways to deal with these problems, and these people. This book will serve as your guide and your handbook to help you as you negotiate these obstacles during your transition from conservative to a productive liberal elite and beyond. Welcome to The Playbook.

Chapter 1

Understanding the Brilliance of Liberalism

If you are reading this book, you have obviously already embraced the idea of becoming a liberal and you want to be the best liberal possible. That's great, you have already taken the first step. However, in order to be the best agent for change possible, we need to make sure that you fully understand liberalism and its ideas, as well as our ties to socialism. Many of those in our movement have begun to adopt the word "Progressive" as a way to indicate that we are moving forward towards socialism. Many times, the term liberal and progressive can almost be used interchangeably.

However, the easiest way to keep yourself on the right path is to simply oppose anything and everything that conservatives and Republicans propose. That's the easy part. Now, let's look a little deeper into what it takes to be a good lefty.

Liberalism is the collective set of ideals that you must embrace in order to help the collective advance our political agenda. You may not agree with, or understand all the stances, but in order to be a good liberal, you must just trust in the intellect of the larger group and adopt these ideas as your own. Just because something doesn't make sense to you, doesn't mean it's wrong.

Use emotion, not logic. The conservatives will constantly try to use logic, facts and actual historical references or examples to prove their point. Don't fall for this trap! We do not need actual data. In fact, progressive thought does not require any actual critical thought at all. That's part of the beauty of the system! It's much easier, and much less work, to simply trust that the progressive ideology is correct and don't worry about the validity of the argument.

It is important to note that we have one of the strongest allies on the planet: the Democratic Party, the DNC. Many of the tactics that we will address have been perfected by the Democrats and their supporters through years of practice. They have totally embraced the idea that this country needs to be fundamentally transformed into a better place where big government can be empowered to manage our daily lives for us. This is tied directly to our principle that the ideas of a larger group must be better than an individual who has been allowed to come up with ideas on his own.

The Democratic National Committee has taken undergone an astounding transformation since the middle of the last century. The group cemented its place in the twentieth century as a group of independent, critical thinking liberals looking out for the common working man. However, over the last several decades the DNC has steadily transitioned to the politburo it is today.

The modern collectivist DNC has a singular focus: achieve and maintain money and power for themselves and those in their circle. This same group has proven that with sufficient power, influence, wealth, intimidation and a willingness to be violent they have virtual impunity to do whatever they want to increase their wealth & power. Of course, these benefits cannot be enjoyed by the everyday citizen. These benefits are reserved for the new aristocracy, the new ruling class, the Liberal Elite.

If we are to be considered a member of this caste, or at least to be in the protected circle of them, we must always show our support for the Democratic Party. If you are ever unsure of what to support, you can typically just wait for them to tell you what your opinions are and then we can all rally around them in a display of solidarity! It is very effective and allows us to best leverage our numbers to affect whatever the party decides is our most important topic of the day.

This will also allow us to redirect public interest away from anything that we don't want in the limelight. In fact, we can pull attention away from anything that might be beneficial to the long-term success of the United States. Understand this: for our progressive agenda of transformation to be truly successful, the United States in its current form MUST fail. Luckily, our Democratic allies have been weakening the country for decades and we just have to keep up the effort!

You must understand that much of being good liberal centers around simply having the right mindset. Adopt the mentality that anything we say is right. Again, it doesn't matter if it makes sense, it just matters that we mindlessly and emphatically parrot whatever the party leaders are claiming is the truth. Assume it is correct. It is easier to maintain the right mindset if you just presume that the party leaders always have the correct information.

Do not fact check anything that we are supporting. There's no point. Luckily the DNC provides plenty of "independent fact-checkers" that are already bought and paid for. This overarching control of the system allows us to discredit essentially anything that we view as a threat. These "neutral" parties provide us with the cover that we need to cover up truths, and the ignorant masses naively believe that they are non-partisan and independent! Luckily for us the general population typically enjoys letting others do their thinking for them. We're happy to oblige.

It is also important to embrace the brilliant ideals of Socialism. At its root, Socialism is the idea that everyone is treated equally and fairly. Who can argue against fairness? Again, don't do any research on Socialism. The history books try to make Socialism look bad by claiming that it always ends up with a ruling class and a poor lower class. They will point out that Socialist societies in the past have imploded and led to mass poverty, starvation and societal collapse. That's not important to us. What is important is that we constantly and incessantly preach that Socialism is about everyone being treated fairly. Any Socialist society that didn't thrive in the past just wasn't trying hard enough to impose equality on the masses. We will be successful, because we are more passionate about forcing everyone to be tolerant of our beliefs than any other people in history.

As Hillary Clinton so brilliantly pointed out: "We must stop thinking of the individual and start thinking about what is best for society."[1] Of course, many will recognize the similarity to Adolph Hitler's famous quote: "Society's needs come before the individual's needs."[2] While it's true that many of our beliefs, actions and political policies align with the teachings of Adolph Hitler, any association with der fuehrer would be negative. Therefore, we simply deny the similarities and continue to accuse the Republicans of acting like Nazis. Don't ever acknowledge these parallels. Simply continue to present our ideas as new, groundbreaking ideas designed to encourage equality and lift the poor out of poverty. As we move through this book, I will point out a few more examples of how we can best utilize the ideas and policies of Adolph Hitler. However, I must reinforce to you, that as a loyal liberal, you must always deny that we are doing this. Since the word Socialism has become acceptable in modern U.S. society, you can always direct the conversation away from any reference to Hitler and towards the policies of a modern, fair Socialist model.

Since you are new to Socialism, let me put your mind at ease. Socialism and equality are good things. However, don't read too much into the whole "equality" part of it. If you do your part and embrace the party line, you will be rewarded in the new Socialist government. One great thing about distributing things equally is that everything that is going to be distributed must first be consolidated. Only then may it be distributed equally to the masses. The vast majority of our ranks will get a small share of the collected money or goods, enough to keep them quiet and keep them in line. We call their "entitlements".

However, as an elite in our Socialist society, your equal part will be better than the other equal parts distributed to the people. That's the great part about being in management. We get to determine what is equal! However, you must, always, stress that EVERYONE is being treated equally and fairly. We'll get into hypocrisy and outright lies later. For now, it's important to understand that you MUST treat whatever our leaders say as the truth. If they say that everyone will get equal amounts of free stuff, then you should emphatically parrot the party's stance. Once you perfect this technique, you'll be well on your way to becoming a great subject.

To prove this point, in 2017 Democratic Socialist, and Presidential candidate Bernie Sanders' website stated: "the issue of wealth and income inequality is the great moral issue of our time, it is the great economic issue of our time, and it is the great political issue of our time." He made over one million dollars that year, which put him in the top 1% of the United States in earnings for the year. (See Chapter 4, Hypocrisy)

In fact, some of the richest people in the country are liberals, and liberal politicians are among some of the richest! First, U.S. Senators make $174,000 per year regardless of how well they do (or do not do) their job. Luckily, that job puts them in a very good position to "negotiate" other things, resulting in some very lucrative endeavors. When you aren't restricted by morals and you play it loose with the law, you can do pretty well for yourself. Let's look at a few examples from the Democratic Party:

Democrat	Estimated net worth in 2018
Nancy Pelosi	$16 million
Barrack Obama	Estimated between $40 million and $242 million
John Kerry	$238.8 million
Dianne Feinstein	$77 million
Hillary Clinton	$45 million

If you want to understand and embrace the Socialist agenda, you must be willing to suspend your common sense and enthusiastically support the idea that confiscating a large percentage of the population's income through taxes is a good idea. This idea supports the overall socialistic model and is a key piece to the bigger picture.

Many of those on the left are highly educated people who have been bombarded with our ideology so effectively, that they not only support it, but they have internalized it. They will stand up and use their intellect, their position of power and their personal influence to impose the party stance onto anyone that they can. To complete your transition to a true believer, you must take the same approach. Embrace the leftist mentality. Make it part of who you are. Then force it on everyone around you.

Chapter 2

Tools of the Trade

We have many tools at our disposal for the conduct of our mission. It is important to be well versed in as many methods and techniques as possible to further our agenda. For this book, we will discuss racism, outrage, hypocrisy, and more. However, these are just the big guns. You must not only understand the tools, but more importantly, you must understand how to use them.

The better you understand these tricks and techniques, the better you will be at manipulating those around you to support our end game. Additionally, this book is organized in a way so that you may use an individual chapter as a reference when recruiting a new person into our folds. After all, this IS a playbook, and it needs to be a usable reference manual. When you are talking to someone about the beauty of liberalism, or the efficiency of Socialism, pay attention to what is important to that person. Then you can reference the part of this book that will be most appealing to that person. It doesn't matter if the person supports all our ideals. Just get them on board with one or two of the ideas and then we can work on getting them to embrace blind faith in the rest of our causes.

This works because many people are single-issue voters. For instance, if you figure out that a person supports gun control, you can harp on the left's anti-gun stance and that may be enough to get this person off the fence and into the socialist camp. Likewise, if you know that a person doesn't make much money, you can point out that we support a higher minimum wage and wealth redistribution. This alone might be enough to get them on board. If that person also happens to be pro-gun, simply forget to mention that we are anti-second amendment. Just point out that Democrats support a higher minimum wage because we "care about the common man."

Use what is important to them to convince them that we are on their side. Then, even if they are pro-gun, their Democratic vote supports our anti-gun agenda. Once they vote Democrat once, they are much more likely to do it again next time. Just look at that guy who has bought four or five vehicles in a row of the same make. People like to have something to stand for or something to believe in. People are naturally creatures of habit. If you can convince someone, or even trick someone into committing to liberalism, there is a good chance that they will stay. This has created an interesting side effect.

Many thousands of our supporters, who have consistently voted for Democratic candidates in very liberal states, particularly California, are now moving to different states to escape the high taxes. However, once they move to the next state with a more agreeable tax code, they then vote for the Democratic candidates in that new location. This has happened in such large numbers that we now see states that were formerly red shifting to blue!

Once you get someone to commit to our side, it's usually easy to keep them there. This is essentially a propaganda campaign being conducted at the lowest levels and at the highest levels simultaneously, and the importance of propaganda cannot be overstated. "Propaganda works best when those who are being manipulated are confident they are acting on their own free will" ~Joseph Goebbels7

One of the most important tenets that we need others to embrace is the notion that government can take care of you better than you can take care of yourself. We can look to California for some great examples of convincing the masses exactly that. In fact, many aspects of the California state government could serve as an example for the national government. For example, the state has steadily increased restrictions on nearly everything you can think of in the name of the "greater good". They have banned things such as plastic shopping bags and plastic drinking straws and the citizens just accept it because both of those items are bad for the environment. While it is true that these items often end up in landfills or even worse, in the ocean, that's not the point here. The point here is to help condition the people of California to having the government regulate EVERY aspect of their lives.

The mainstream (leftist) media is clearly on our side and will celebrate this move as being good for the environment. Any right-leaning media outlets will criticize it as an invasive, ineffective, over-reaching measure with no actual effect on the environment. Both are correct. It can, in theory, reduce the amount of plastic being moved into trash or recycling. However, the effect will be infinitesimal with no actual measurable effect. Once again, not the point. As these two sides of the aisle argue back and forth about the effectiveness of the legislation, the focus is being diverted from the actual intent of the law, which is to pass yet another behavior controlling regulation.

With every unnecessary or overreaching law that California passes, the people get more and more accustomed to having their daily lives dictated to them. This is a HUGE win for liberalism, and an important step towards Socialism. As we continue to move our progressive agenda forward, we want as many people as possible to get accustomed to just rolling over and taking whatever abuse, ridiculous tax, restriction or unconstitutional control measures we put on them. Most people will. The more we get them conditioned to it, the easier it will be to pass more and more restrictive laws. We will slowly take complete control of them, and most won't even notice it happening.

I liken it to the old tale of how to catch a wild hog: There was once a farmer who had a problem with wild hogs tearing up his crops. He found a place near his fields where he could see that the hogs had been rooting around in the dirt. The farmer built a fence in a straight line and baited the area on one side with food. When the hogs found the food, they didn't pay attention to the fence. They just ate the food. The farmer continued to place food by the fence to get the hogs accustomed to being fed there. Then he added another side of the fence, so the fenced area was shaped like a giant "L", and he kept feeding the hogs. The hogs got accustomed to this fence too.

Then the farmer added the other side, creating a giant "U" shape. Once again, the hogs got accustomed to the inconvenience of going around this fence because they got free food. After a while, the farmer put the fourth and final side of the fence up, enclosing the area, but leaving an open gate in the middle of this last side. At first, the hogs were hesitant, but smelling the food, they became bolder and went through the open gate to get at the food. The farmer observed the hogs from a concealed position. Once the hogs were inside, he pulled a hidden rope, slamming the gate closed on the fence. He had captured the hogs by slowly getting them used to a more and more restrictive environment. This is the technique we are using effectively against the American public. Many Californians have gotten so accustomed to fences that they won't even notice when the Democratic government closes the gate on them.

The bulk of American people can be manipulated just like the hogs in the story. As a matter of fact, I often compare the American public to a herd of livestock. We, as liberals, have the responsibility to herd these animals and guide them in their daily lives. Most people just want to live their lives and have the daily conveniences that we have come to expect in this country. This works in our favor. People can generally be pacified by simply giving them something to distract them from the fact that we are taxing them for more than they are getting, or slowly eroding their personal liberties.

As we work to take over America completely, we must always keep the common citizen busy with useless, mind-numbing distractions that prevent them from paying attention to what we are actually doing. We use things like idiot celebrities who are inconsequential or past their prime and will do anything to stay in the spotlight. These nearly forgotten "celebrities" are more than happy to stand up and preach for us, just to get another fifteen minutes in the spotlight. Even though they may be insignificant in the entertainment world, they should still be viewed as useful pawns to manipulate those who still put value in the opinions of people just because they were once on television or in a movie.

For example, we've had a useful idiot hold up a mock severed bloody head of then-President Trump. This was obviously meant to plant the idea that the president should be murdered. It was great! It got an enormous amount of attention even though the C-list actress later issued an apology. It didn't matter, because the seed had already been planted. See Chapter 4 Hypocrisy, and Chapter 11 Violence.

This technique has proven so effective that it has attracted the attention of more current celebrities. We understand that celebrities can be manipulated just like anyone else in the ignorant, brainwashed masses, and we must take advantage of this fact. Generally speaking, people will put credence in the beliefs and recommendations of these celebrities. This person could be an actor or athlete or essentially anyone who has managed to make it onto television for any reason. It doesn't matter.

The public will assign importance to the words of these people, so we need to keep them on the talking points. It doesn't matter if an athlete is the most idiotic, uneducated, unthinking imbecile on the planet. In fact, that's actual preferable. If a player can dribble a basketball and win games, people will assign some inherent value to his (or her) "opinions". That's great! We just have to tell them what their "opinions" will be, and they can help push the party's agenda along.

If you expect to ever truly become a liberal elite, you MUST embrace the idea that the ruling class is inherently smarter than the masses. That is why we can use these methods successfully against these simpletons. Keep in mind that oftentimes, the masses include famous or influential people. However, just because they are famous, doesn't mean that they are smart. In fact, some of our most successful pawns for spreading our message are some of the least intelligent members of our ranks. As the brilliant Joseph Goebbels once said "...the rank and file are usually much more primitive than we imagine. Propaganda must therefore always be essentially simple and repetitious."3

These celebrities are a useful tool that must be manipulated effectively. Just because they currently have money and influence, doesn't mean that they are automatically accepted into the ranks of ruling class. We, as the intellectual leadership of the movement, will decide who makes the cut and who will be reduced to just another cog in the wheel of our Socialist machine. This just highlights the importance of talent management. Use the person in the best way possible to support the big picture. Once they cease to be influential, they can be discarded along with anyone else that we can no longer exploit.

Pushing our agenda must be a continuous, ongoing process if we expect to be successful. Luckily, we have the greatest 24 hour a day propaganda delivery system in history, the television.

Since we have liberals in charge of most television networks, we can continue to drive our narrative with a tidal wave of shows that either distract the masses or actively work towards brainwashing the viewers with our propaganda. We use popular shows to quietly and slowly indoctrinate the viewers into accepting our version of reality as normal. Once again, we follow the lead of Joseph Goebbels. He once said, "This is the secret of propaganda: Those who are to be persuaded by it should be completely immersed in the ideas of the propaganda, without ever noticing that they are being immersed in it."4

We have a very good example to highlight the effectiveness of this technique. In a 2015 Gallup reported that only 3.8% of Americans identify as gay, lesbian or bisexual. However, a separate Gallup poll (2013) revealed that many Americans guessed that number to be as much as 23%!5

This is a great example of the success of our propaganda efforts. In an effort to push our agenda with the LGBT community (and more importantly, the voters who support LGBT), we push having gays and transgender in every television show or movie possible. This overrepresentation of a certain demographic leads people to assume that there are more than there actually are. We don't just stop at gays, lesbians and bisexuals though. As a matter of fact, we want to exploit as much of the LGBTQIAPK community as possible. One of the easiest ways to do this is to act like we accept them no matter how outrageous their claims or actions.

Our acceptance of them works in our favor in two different ways. Firstly, as mentioned above, it is helpful to our voter base. Many people in the gay community are single issue voters, so we can get them and anyone supporting the gay community to vote for us, even if they don't believe in anything else that we are pushing. Secondly, as the beliefs, actions and sexual practices become more and more outrageous, this helps us to continue to destroy the outdated moral fabric of the United States.

This is not "Leave it to Beaver" anymore. We need to embrace, even encourage deviant behavior in our communities, and continue to insist that this behavior is normal. Anyone that says it isn't acceptable can quickly be branded as "intolerant", shunned and even "cancelled".

One brilliant example is the abuse and exploitation of children. We have conditioned the masses to accept and even praise the abuse of children. One of the most notable current illustrations is the case of a young autistic boy who has gained fame within the drag queen circles. When the child was only eleven years old, he stated that he could not remember ever wearing boy's clothing. He was convinced at an early age (too young to make his own decisions) that he was gay, or "gender fluid". His mother has since promoted him shamelessly and paraded him around like a common circus attraction in an effort to profit from his condition. She even took him to adult gay bars at the age of eleven and had him dance for the gay men while they threw money at him like a common stripper.

All the while, the mainstream media has praised this behavior as "acceptance" and "tolerance". RuPaul referred to him as "the future of America."20 This scenario helps us in three distinct ways. Firstly, it helps us advance the common mentality towards the deconstruction of the moral fabric that was established by the ridiculous Christian beliefs of the past. Secondly, it is already conditioning this child to vote for all left leaning politicians in the future, since they are "supporting" gay initiatives.

Finally, because this child has been established as a "role model" for other young people, it will help encourage other children to vote for us in the future as well. The mental health of this child is a small price to pay. He should be viewed as just another pawn and his wellbeing is unimportant as long as we can use him in the advancement of our agenda.

As progressive thinkers, we must consistently push this departure from traditional beliefs of right and wrong. The morals that have been accepted as the social norm of the United States for the last two and half centuries MUST be ridiculed as outdated and non-applicable to the 21st century. These beliefs are one of the primary reasons America is still standing today. If we are going to tear down America and rebuild it as a progressive, utopian socialist society, then these ideals must be abolished. Embrace the radical. Embrace the mentally ill and call it normal. Condemn old fashioned morals as outdated. Say that they are unable to evolve, and point out that a failure to evolve leads to extinction.

Use any method or approach possible to tear at the foundation that the conservatives cling to. Be outrageous! Be loud! Be shocking! We are even supporting a movement that is trying to reclassify pedophilia as a natural sexual orientation! 6 You may think that we don't stand a chance. However, there was a time, not to long ago, when homosexuality was called a mental illness. Now it is celebrated, exalted and hailed as heroic! We'll keep tirelessly pushing our agenda and create a "new normal" until all our beliefs are considered commonplace. Don't concern yourself with the irreparable damage being done to the children. Once again, suspend common sense and just call it "tolerance". We'll talk more about tolerance in Chapter 4, Hypocrisy.

Earlier in this chapter, I mentioned that Americans often act with a herd mentality. This is especially true of the American youth. They believe what they are told and will even be outraged if you tell them that they should be outraged. As you advance towards becoming a liberal elite, never forget that these sheep are a great weapon.

This herd may be driven towards the conservatives in a stampede that can be used to crush our enemy. For example, let's look at the Antifa movement. The Antifa crowd claims that they are "Anti-Fascist". However, if you look at the definition of fascism, they are acting EXCACTLY as fascists. This is great!

This is exactly what we want. We have used the media (and social media) to whip these gullible idealists into frenzy and we can throw them at whatever group or cause we want. Then just sit back and watch the carnage. It's a beautiful thing. They are literally the embodiment of what they are protesting against, but they are so ignorant that they don't even know it! The Antifa movement takes advantage of several things that are working in our favor right now. Firstly, young people are usually idealistic, but have very little life experience. Secondly, they are easily manipulated and enraged. Thirdly, since they were children, they've been told that they are "special" and that they "deserve" this or that, so they feel entitled.

However, don't be fooled into thinking that our Antifa machine is just made up of uneducated kids living in their mother's basements, as many people try to claim. Our propaganda effort of promoting "social justice" has been so overwhelmingly successful that the ranks of Antifa have swollen with plenty of white, middle class (and sometimes upper class), educated young people. We have been so successful that even our left-wing teachers and professors have donned black hoodies and joined the rank and file of our militant arm.

Probably the most beautiful thing about our Antifa foot soldiers is that they are expendable. If they get arrested, injured or killed, it doesn't matter to us. All that matters is that we can take advantage of their actions to further our cause. Plus, if we are lucky enough to get some of them killed, we can act like we care and leverage the death into yet more outrage! It works even better if the ones that are killed are black, then we can throw racism into the mix as well. It's good to kill other minorities as well, but history has shown that we liberals can get the most mileage out of killing a young black kid.

That leads to "outrage" and beating the drums and blaming the right once again, and that leads to more recruitment and the cycle continues. It's wonderful and these stupid kids fall for it over and over again. It's a beautiful, destructive hurricane of events that serves us like a slave.

Chapter 3

Racism and Other Useful Discriminatory Practices

We want to bring up racism very early in this book because this is one of our most used tools as a liberal. One might even call this our "Go to" response to conservative arguments. We are not concerned about whether racism is good or bad. That is irrelevant. What is important is how we can best utilize it to push our agenda on the American public.

Racism can be used in two primary ways. The first and easiest way to use racism to our advantage is to claim something is racist to delegitimize or undermine anything that the conservatives or Republicans are doing. As an example, anything that has to do with the security of the country, we can just call it racist because it may or may not affect people of different races. Actually, it doesn't even matter if they are of a different race. We can still yell "Racism!" if it affects anyone that we want to support. For example, many Americans are trying to unjustly close off the borders to the United States. We can call it racism against Latinos or Mexicans or whoever we think we can use as a political pawn or voter in the future.

Maybe an action isn't affecting a race at all, but it's affecting a religion, a political group, a left-leaning faction or a certain economic class. We don't need to concern ourselves that it isn't a race. We can still yell

"Racism" and shame the conservatives into backing down. We can literally cry racism at any slight that we want to. Simply be "outraged" at the discrimination and throw racism into it as well (See Chapter 6, Outrage and The Victim Mentality). For example, if a law, regulation or policy that is supported by the Republicans might affect a portion of a community that happens to have some Muslims in it, that's great! We can claim that the Republicans are targeting Muslims, committing religious discrimination and they are RACIST!

Just simply throw the word "racist" on the end of any argument to help strengthen your stance and exert your moral superiority. Conservatives and especially Christians are scared of the word and will be forced to abandon their other arguments to defend themselves from the allegations of racism. Honesty, it's pathetic that they still fall for this ruse!

We have overused this ploy for so many years, that it is amazing that it still works! However, we have many warriors out in the field who keep stirring the pot of racial unrest. Many of our most effective agitators hide behind the facade of being clergymen. They refer to themselves as "Reverend" or "Pastor". This adds legitimacy in the eyes of many people, including the enemy, many of whom still place importance in the ideals of Christianity.

It makes them less likely to fight back against the claims of these individuals because they don't want to be perceived as going against the church! These "clergy" can spew hate, division and fan the flames of racism and racial division, while simultaneously claiming to fight racism. It's brilliant!

This racial unrest on a national level is important if we want to be able to continue to use racism as a tool to undermine the capitalistic advancements of this country and keep us moving towards our goals. It is understood that sometimes there will be casualties as a result of our actions. This is completely acceptable, and even desirable. As we go about setting blacks against whites, or Latinos against whites, or specific nationalities against whites, sometimes there will be violent clashes. These clashes are very useful.

Whenever there is a violent encounter, we, as liberals, should hope for as much bloodshed, suffering and death as possible. "Why?" you ask? Because we can put our spin on it, no matter which side bleeds.

If a minority is the injured party, we can scream "Racism!" and use it to support whatever our most important agenda of the day is. If they were killed or injured while in the conduct of criminal activity, just ignore that aspect of the incident and claim that they were targeted because of their race. If they have a history of crime, downplay it and just claim that they were forced into a life of crime by the oppressive environment cultivated by the rich white people and their white privilege. This is still not their fault.

Put their family members on TV and only show young, innocent looking pictures of them. For instance, if a black man with facial tattoos from prison is killed by police while he was committing armed robbery, just show his little league picture with a video of his mother crying. We've been using this trick for a while now and it's great. Quite honestly, we liberals should hope for as many minorities to be killed as possible. It gives us some great ammunition!

Our most obvious success story is the death of George Floyd. His death has provided us with an enormous amount of power, money and opportunity. From the time of his death, we immediately began capitalizing on it. Our people encouraged looting, which made many of our mindless followers happy because they were able to steal with impunity.

I want to pause here in this section to point out an important facet of human psychology. There are many people in our society that only follow the rules because of the threat of punishment. Once we took away the risk of punishment, they simply began acting the way that they wanted to behave all along. They reverted to a more primitive, tribal, violent behavior. They destroyed property, stole whatever they wanted, attacked police and the symbols of the police such as their cars. I wanted to take the time to point this out because it highlights one of our strongest tools, the mob. The simpletons that we employ as our foot soldiers are very easily manipulated into behaving as savages by using mob mentality to induce their feeling of invincibility.

Let's return now the subject of getting people killed or injured. If the injured or killed parties are white, conservative or Christian, we can call ourselves the victims for having to defend ourselves against these "aggressors". Highlight that our supporters are now having to deal with the pain created by the enemy and that WE are the TRUE victims here. If our liberal puppets were the aggressors that initiated the conflict, once again, just ignore that and deflect the responsibility onto those that we killed or injured.

If there is video evidence, ensure that it is edited in a way that hides our guilt and only shows the parts of the altercation that we can utilize to make the actual victims look like the aggressors. Our allies in the media have been doing this for us for years and sometimes completely change the pictures or videos to support our narrative.

The other obvious additional benefit to this violence is that white people get killed or injured. They are the enemies of our advancement. Don't worry if you're white too. We have another tool called Hypocrisy that will serve you well. We'll address that in the next chapter. When you use hypocrisy in conjunction with appropriate posturing and a thick coat of pandering, your whiteness will be fine.

Regardless of who is hurt, put crying children in the spotlight. However, before you put them in front of cameras, make sure that they are going to say our version of the truth. They MUST reference white oppression, or America's systemic racism, or some other storyline that supports our narrative. Also, don't always assume that children can lie effectively.

Practice with them BEFORE the cameras are rolling so that they remember which parts to lie about and when they can be truthful. Manipulate the children to make them believe what we need them to believe. Too many times in the past, we have seen our comrades try to use children to support our propaganda efforts, only to be undermined when the little bastard told the truth in front of the camera! We CANNOT allow this, except, of course, when the truth happens to be beneficial to us.

The second way that we can use Racism as a tool is more difficult to understand, but arguably more effective in the long game. We can use racism by simply BEING racists! I know that this may sound counterintuitive, but it is exceedingly effective when properly matched with outrage and lies (See Chapter 6, Outrage and the Victim Mentality and Chapter 12, Misdirection and Outright Lies). Our allies in the DNC have been using this technique for decades with continued success, so we will continue to abuse whatever group we need to, as long as it supports our goals.

However, one constant is that you must consistently and openly discriminate against whites. Support any policy, program or group that excludes white people. For example, if a group wants to create a college fund for "Underprivileged African Americans", that is something we can support as long as it actively discriminates against Caucasians. However, if you see a program that does not discriminate against whites, claim that minorities are underrepresented and accuse them of being racist. For example, if a program is designed to help poor Appalachian families, we should not support it, since that area of the country does not have as many black or Latino future voters. You may be wondering how this policy helps further our cause. It helps us because it weakens the whites while simultaneously ingratiating us to the black voter base and those who vote to support the black community.

The second half of that sentence is what is actually important; "those who support the black community". We liberals don't ACTUALLY care about blacks. Sure, their numbers at the voting booth are helpful. However, what is really helpful is all of the giant groups of white people that want to prove how tolerant and accepting they are by helping the poor, underprivileged, uneducated "people of color".

Those are some numbers that are big enough to swing elections (for elections that we can't just outright rig). Take advantage of this desire. Pander to them. Pretend to care about the things that they care about. Let's look at a great example. In 2007, Hillary Clinton was speaking at a black church and tried to ingratiate herself to the group. As an intellectual powerhouse, she knew that the uneducated blacks in the church would not recognize that she was simply pandering to them as she attempted to assume what she thought was a stereotypical black accent and quoted a song by the late Reverend James Cleveland, considered by many to be the father of black gospel music: "I don't feel no ways tired..."

She went on to quote more of the lyrics and even went as far as to use a quote of Saint Paul from the bible after that. Now obviously, it is unlikely that she was familiar with either of these quotes prior to her speech writers preparing her for that day. However, this was an excellent example of how a white person can overcome their whiteness to be a force for manipulating minorities to vote the way we need them to.

Now, obviously we cannot be caught using any kind of racial or ethnic slur since that would alienate some of our subjects, and potentially cost us at the voting booth. However, we continue to embrace and use the methodology of Franklin Delano Roosevelt: We should look like an answer to a problem. As long as our liberal "solutions" appear to be beneficial to the minority communities or provide them with some sort of reward, we can continue to expect their support.

If we can't find any problems, we can just invent the problem and then "solve" the problem for them by getting them some money or something else that they find attractive. For a good example of this, just look back at the brilliant program by President Obama to give out free cell phones. Create the illusion of a problem by pointing it out. Then fund the "solution" which provides people with something that will ingratiate them to our cause. It was quite brilliant. It did absolutely nothing to help the lower class improve their situation, but it made it look like we were helping them! It made it look as if we care. Brilliant! We liberals are so much smarter than the minority community as a whole, that they won't even know that we are manipulating them, and they will continue to vote for us. But, as President Roosevelt suggested, don't give them too much.

You may not feel that the President Roosevelt reference is relevant in today's society. After all, he was president in the 1930's and 1940's, which was pre-civil rights era. So, let's look at some more modern examples. Obviously, President Joe Biden has given us many examples that we can use. For example, in 2019 Mr. Biden said in a speech that "Poor kids are just as bright and just as talented as white kids."8

This was quickly dismissed as an apparent gaffe by the then presidential candidate. However, we know the truth. The truth is that he accidentally said what he was actually thinking. Look, as liberal elites, we know that we are superior, smarter and more deserving than the average plebian servant in our society, and that is fine. It's just reality. However, we need to guard against being truthful about it in public. It is difficult to virtue signal and act like we are trying to help someone other than ourselves, while simultaneously being truthful.

Some might argue that the minorities are not enough of a voter base to worry about. After all, they are, by definition, less numerous than the whites. However, pandering to the blacks and Latinos will attract the self-righteous whites that will vote for anything that looks like it might be pro-minority. This group is desperate to project the "I'm not a racist" image to their friends and family. As a result, they will willingly vote for any person or legislation that will support this facade.

Speaking of pandering, let's look at the wonderful stunt staged by Nancy Pelosi and Chuck Schumer in June of 2020 following the death of George Floyd. The speaker showed her tremendous leadership by bringing together a group of Democratic lawmakers for this brilliant exercise in pandering.

Let me reiterate that we never admit to the public that it's pandering, it's just a continuing effort of solidarity to show how much we "care" about the poor minorities in our country. The Speaker of the House and a host of Democrats gathered in Emancipation Hall in the US Capital for an amazing, staged photo op. The choice of locations was brilliant, and they knelt for the same amount of time that the former police officer knelt on George Floyd during his arrest.

The symbolism was thick as they wore African Kente cloths (sometimes worn in Ghana) in a multi-faceted display of solidarity with the African American community and specifically the Black Lives Matter group. Obviously if any conservatives did this, we would call it outrageous and accuse them of cultural appropriation, but that doesn't affect us. (See chapter 4, Hypocrisy, and Chapter 6, Outrage and the Victim Mentality)

When fooling the ignorant minorities, do not be too confrontational with them, especially if you're white. For another example of how NOT to do things, we can once again look to President Biden. When he was running for president, he was allowed to do an interview with an African American radio personality in NY and made the statement: "If you have a problem figuring out if you're for me or Trump, then you ain't black."9 He even laughed a little after he said it. This is not what we want to be doing. It was too obvious that he wasn't taking the situation seriously. At the time, it was right in the middle of the George Floyd riots. The black community was already angry and we were trying to garner support for an old white man with a history of stereotyping and insulting the black community. It was the perfect opportunity to pander and make promises that we have no intention of keeping.

Instead, he squandered the chance and actually ended up hurting his stance with many of the listeners. Now, obviously, by that point, Mr. Biden probably already knew that he was going to win the election, so he wasn't overly concerned with "winning the black vote". However, we can't operate on the assumption that we will always be able to steal elections in the future. We must stay vigilant and keep up the show, just in case.

Now, earlier, I said that we should not use ethnic or racial slurs. There is an exception to this rule. It is completely acceptable to discriminate or insult whites or anything associated with Christianity and in most cases Jews. As a matter of fact, we should take every opportunity possible to tear down whites or Christians. Mainstream television, movies, and especially the media are very helpful in this because they constantly push an anti-Christian agenda in nearly every venue. Christianity is an easy target. Any time a conservative references a Christian value in an argument, you can roll your eyes and insinuate that they are stupid. Simply dismiss it as superstition or compare it to science fiction (See Chapter 7, Smug Intellectualism). I'll give you some examples.

If a conservative argues against mass government distribution of funds, you can accuse them of not supporting charity, which is in the bible. If they want to support the right of private citizens to have firearms, tell them that their bible says "Thou shalt not kill". If they speak of love or caring for their neighbor, then just point out that those are liberal ideas! Just twist whatever they say in a manner so that it supports our cause. If they make an argument that you can't defeat, you can always fall back to screaming at them and by the end of the conversation figure out a way to call them a racist. Then you can just throw your hands up in mock disgust and refuse to talk to them because they are a racist or "unbelievable". This gets you out of an argument that you were going to lose and lets you claim the moral high ground.

To help support our blitzkrieg-style approach to racism, we have entered a relatively new player into the game, critical race theory (CRT). I say relatively new, because its roots are in the late 1980s, but we are only now realizing its full potential. CRT is actually pretty overt in its approach to crying racism. It has roots in the Marxist "critical theory". It essentially claims that the United States is built around a White Supremacy model and that society, culture and even the laws are all designed to keep the minorities in check and promote advancement for whites.

CRT is going to be a big player in upcoming years, because it not only consolidates many of our claims, but it is generally believed by millions of people! They actually believe that the mean white lawmakers in Washington are sitting around at night thinking of ways to write laws that will specifically target non-whites, (especially blacks) while simultaneously lifting up white citizens! The idea of CRT is directly linked to the victim mentality mentioned in this chapter. However, it is much more, so much more.

Many of the tenets of CRT are racist in their nature. However, that isn't important to us. What is important is how we can use this tool to continue to drive the wedge into the United States that will eventually result in the destruction of the country. Again, keep in mind that as good liberals, we must support destroying the old school America if we are going to be able to continue to build the new, utopian, Socialist America. If you keep focused, stay the course as a liberal elite, you can be a part of this ruling class that will have power, riches and influence, just like the liberal elites in all the other Socialist countries in the world.

So, you may be asking "How can I use CRT as a tool to destroy America?" That's a great question, so let's look at some of the tenets of CRT, so we can see how to best utilize them. First, (and I know it's ridiculous, but stay with me here) CRT claims that race isn't even based in biology. Race is merely a social construct, created by powerful white men. You must embrace the idea that the laws of the United States and even the entire legal institution is inherently racist. In fact, since most laws were written by white men, they MUST have been invented to advance the position of whites and keep down the minorities, especially blacks. As was pointed out earlier, do not worry about finding any actual evidence or truth to our claims.

Obviously, we know that when the laws were written, they were not intended to target one race over another. However, ignore that truth and embrace the stance that the laws are racially motivated and therefore MUST be unjust. This will support the CRT, encourage the blacks to support our cause and keep those whites voting our way so they can prove how non-racist they are.

Speaking of non-racist, another aspect of the Critical Race Theory which will be especially destructive (and therefore useful to us) is the idea that simply not being racist is insufficient. You must be actively "non-racist". What is this? This is the idea that everyone must actively analyze every scenario and interaction for anything that might possibly be construed as having a racial motivation or undertone.

Essentially, if there is any way possible to twist any scenario, speech or situation in such a manner that it could be forced to be interpreted as racist, then it should be considered racist! It doesn't matter if it was completely innocent, and no racist motivations were present. This one technique allows us to insert racism where there was no racist intent. Just as we discussed in chapter one, facts are not important. What is important is that we can take advantage of each and every situation and manipulate them to our benefit.

However, this is only the first step. Once we have forcefully invented the "racism", we can now demand action! We can demand legislation, or compensation, or whatever we need at the time. We can use this false racism to compel action where no action was actually needed. Wonderful! Earlier in this chapter, we addressed white people trying to prove how "not racist" they are. This is the perfect tool to facilitate that effect.

Another great facet of the Critical Race Theory is that none of the negative aspects of racism can be applied to blacks. Essentially it allows blacks, and to a lesser extent, other people of color, to act in an overtly racist manner and they get a free pass. We have seen a recent surge in exclusionary organizations and that move is being embraced and even celebrated: Black only TV shows, black only dating sights, black only organizations, black only charities etc. Let's take a moment and look at the brilliance of this movement. If we were to do any of that with whites, it would immediately be attacked as a "white supremacy" organization! Can you imagine a charity that openly stated that it was only going to support white children and non-white children were not eligible? There would be a nuclear explosion of attacks on that organization! The sanctimonious American public would "cancel" that organization and probably sue them out of existence, if not burn their offices down. Yet the practice of discriminating against whites is encouraged and even heralded as a position of virtue!

You can probably see that the discussion on the Critical Race Theory could just as easily fit into Chapter 6, Outrage and the Victim Mentality since one of columns supporting CRT is embracing and highlighting how everything is unfair for the African American community in general. In other words, it encourages playing the victim. However, I chose to put it here since the primary end state of teaching Critical Race Theory will be to promote racism, division and ultimately destroy the advancements in race relations made in the last sixty years. Honestly, CRT will be so useful in destroying the status quo of the U.S. culture that it could have its own chapter. No, its own book. However, in the interest of keeping this handbook brief, let's look at another great tool, xenophobia.

Xenophobia is the fear of foreigners or things that are foreign. If you can't quite stuff the word "racism" into a sentence, you can shift gears and call the conservative xenophobic. It works great in nearly any argument, and much like the term "racist", the conservatives will often abandon whatever you were arguing about just to defend against this new accusation. Additionally, many people don't even know what it means, but they know it's bad, so they will automatically start trying to defend themselves. It's great!

We need to have a good understanding of the overall effectiveness of racism and these other discriminatory practices because they form the basis for one of the pillars of our success: division of the American people. We must always strive to maintain the population divided against itself. It is a basic principle of maintaining control of a people. If we can succeed in keeping the citizens divided and pitched against one another, they are unable to unite against us and the party. In this aspect of the plan, we are using multiple tools; racism, hate, hypocrisy, essentially anything that we can to maintain strife and disunion in the United States.

One of the worst things that could happen to us would be for the citizenry to unite, get along and start analyzing our actions. If the citizens of the country were to ever stand up as one voice and hold us accountable for our actions, our castle would crumble. Luckily for us, we have been so effective at brainwashing and lying to the masses for so long, that the generally accepted attitude in the United States is that racism is increasing rather than decreasing. Arguably, it is. Thanks to our valiant effort.

Despite our successful efforts of advancing racism and the resultant division within the country, we must continue to relentlessly push the agenda and prevent any healing amongst the general population. Remember, the rule of thumb for making racism an effective weapon in this war for America is to use it liberally and often, regardless of situation or scenario. We understand that sometimes, it's hard to force racism into an argument when the subject is clearly not racist. However, keep doing so. We cannot let this wonderful tool go to waste. Since our incessant push of racism is such a hypocritical act, this is a great segue into our next chapter, hypocrisy.

Chapter 4

Hypocrisy

It's hard to say which of our tools are the most effective. However, it's not hard to see which ones we use the most. Hypocrisy is certainly one of our most used weapons, right up there with racism. The reason for that is because we can use it in conjunction with so many of the other tools in our toolbox. To be fair, most of the tools that we are talking about in this book are typically in conjunction with other techniques. For example, our use of racism is, by definition, hypocritical, because we claim to be championing the minorities, while actually exploiting them.

However, that's fine. Many of the techniques MUST incorporate hypocrisy to be effective. For example, we will oppose anything a Republican President says, even if our Democratic Presidents have said the exact same thing in recent years. A great recent example was our all-out assault on the former Republican President Trump for his stance that we should enforce the immigration laws of our country and build a wall along the southern border.

We just ignore the fact that Democratic Presidents Clinton and Obama made speeches with very similar language during their presidencies. In fact, President Obama made numerous speeches and conducted several interviews in which he openly condemned illegal immigration. Even more recently, during a pre-election interview, then-Senator Kamala Harris highly criticized the American border policies under President Trump as a "Human Rights Violation". After being elected to the Vice Presidency, (in her first foreign trip), she directly told those south of the border "Do not come."39

President Bill Clinton, in his 1995 State of the Union Address called for stronger borders, spoke of hiring more border guards and cracking down on illegal hiring. He was even proud to say that his administration had deported twice as many "criminal aliens" than earlier administrations.10 Chuck Schumer, Nancy Pelosi and even President Barrack H. Obama called for many of the same things that Donald Trump supported during his presidency. In 2007, then Senator Obama, in a speech on the senate floor, called for "stronger enforcement on the border and at the workplace."

At the time, Democrats applauded these stances. However, you must keep in mind that neither Clinton nor Obama had any intention of following through with these claims, and we knew that. We knew that these speeches were just political maneuvering, and that's okay.

The problem is that President Trump actually intended to do what he claimed he would do. He was genuinely trying to strengthen the national borders of the United States and enforce the laws of the country. We simply CANNOT allow this! These illegals are all potential future Democratic voters and are very easily manipulated with entitlement programs.

So, we opposed him and accused him of being racist, or xenophobic or any other insult that we could find to help destabilize his position. In order to do all this, all we had to do was ignore the earlier statements by our own party.

Obviously, this is hypocritical. How could we support something that was touted by two Democratic presidents and then turn around and oppose the same policies when they are proposed by a Republican President? It's easy, we just claim that we have evolved with the times and accuse the Republicans of clinging to archaic ideas and outdated policies. We can use this approach to gloss over any situation when we are being called out for our hypocrisy. Claim that we are being progressive and modern and allowing our beliefs to evolve with modern culture, while the Republicans are just recycling old, stale, failed policies from the past.

However, we cannot allow the conservatives to use this same defense. If they allow their policies to evolve, you must accuse them of shifting their positions for purely political reasons and declare that they are lying. You have to appreciate the artistry of this; we are literally being hypocritical when we accuse them of hypocrisy! Beautiful! Force them to defend their new position and then refuse to accept their answers. It doesn't matter if they are telling the truth. As a good liberal, you must never let the truth get in your way.

This leads into the idea of obstructionist politics. As a faithful liberal, we must oppose anything and everything that the Conservatives or Republicans are supporting. It doesn't matter if it's good for the country or not. Once again, this is irrelevant. All that matters is that we oppose everything they do. This will reinforce the national divide that President Obama so brilliantly and seamlessly resurrected, and it will give our elected officials ammunition to use against the Republicans. Furthermore, we now have bold and brave elected officials who are willing to openly call for violence and even hope for murder! When Donald Trump was still president, Missouri state senator Maria Chappelle-Nadal reportedly wrote in her personal social media feed "I hope Trump is assassinated!"11 Nothing ever happened to her. This fact should embolden other liberals to encourage violence as well, since we can see that we will not be punished for it.

We also have great warriors like Frederica Wilson and even more so Maxine Waters, who actively encouraged citizens to harass and confront members of the Trump administration if they saw them. The great thing about this is that people look up to these women and will take their advice. Because of this, these elected officials can use their words as a catalyst to manipulate the citizens (foot soldiers) to go do things which may lead to public fights and (hopefully) eventually even more violent acts. (See Chapter 11, Violence).

If we can get these confrontations to elevate to violence, then we can again capitalize on the situation to exploit whoever is hurt or killed. Then, if our liberal politicians get any political blow back following the encounter, they can just backpedal, twist their own words and lie their way out of it, business as usual. (See Chapter 12, Misdirection and Outright Lies)

You must convey your hypocrisy with a self-righteous flourish that makes it appear as if you genuinely believe your own lies. This is important for maintaining our credibility with the public. Although most of the time it won't matter if your argument is believable or not because if we have done our jobs effectively, the uneducated masses will simply do what they are told and follow the party lines no matter how ridiculous our stances. But do not count on this, as this will lead you into complacency. If we are to bring this country down and transform it into the socialist future that we are pursuing, then we need to control the people, and steer their beliefs and goals in the direction that we need them to go. Therefore, make your hypocritical stances believable and be adamant in your position. This is especially important when the conservatives offer up a logical argument. Your position may be completely ridiculous, but do not back down. Hold your ground. Cut them off when they try to answer and don't let them finish their sentences. If they still try to argue, yell, scream, talk over them and try to make them look foolish. Then call them a racist.

If you embrace hypocrisy and you learn to wield it like a weapon, you will be able to disarm the conservatives' use of constitutionally guaranteed freedoms. The freedoms guaranteed in the Constitution of the United States are dangerous and we must be able to neuter the Bill of Rights if we expect to be successful. For example, let's look at the first amendment. The first amendment actually addresses several different things, but since Americans are typically uneducated about their own constitutional rights, many people think that it just addresses the freedom of speech. We can claim protection under the first amendment for anything we want to promote, even if we know it to be false.

If the conservatives try to shut down our lies, we can threaten to sue them for violating our first amendment right to free speech. Conversely, anytime they say something, we need to attempt to take away their protection of the 1st Amendment. We can just claim that it is "hate speech" and therefore not protected by the 1st Amendment. Hypocrisy at its best. Adolph Hitler put it perfectly when he said "We have to put a stop to the idea that it is a part of everybody's civil rights to say whatever he pleases."12 That is just inspiring.

This ties into our version of "tolerance". We need to actively bait the conservatives into arguments by forcing completely ridiculous claims down their throats and waiting for them to push back. For example, it's helpful to our liberal cause to exploit the mentally ill and encourage their illnesses rather than offer treatment. One way that we can do that is that we should encourage people to continue to invent new genders. When the conservatives do not accept our new invention, we can scream "intolerance!" and draw them into a fight. We can make up dozens or hundreds or an infinite number of genders!

Not only will it drive them crazy, it's quite entertaining for us when they make the same stale "Two Gender" argument over and over again every time we introduce another invented gender! Ignore science and stand fast in your belief that every imaginary gender is real and deserves to be recognized with equality. Claim that they are incapable of comprehending our enlightened understanding of modern gender. Accuse them of being intolerant, while at the same time, you must maintain your complete intolerance of their beliefs.

Another humorous example is to take advantage of someone with clinical lycanthropy, which is when a person believes they are an animal (such as a cat). Obviously, this person needs treatment. However, do not even acknowledge that anything is wrong. Simply claim that the mentally ill person "identifies" as a cat, and if the conservative doesn't accept them, well they are clearly being "intolerant" of that person's right to be a cat! Again, just have fun with this. It's great fun to come up with outrageous new claims. We must act like we believe these claims are real and then sit back and watch the conservatives take the bait and tell us how we are wrong. Now scream "intolerance"! Another funny sidenote to this ploy is that our uneducated masses of gullible liberal followers will actually fall for this as well and take up the cause of protecting the "rights of the furries!" Hilarious! Useful idiots can be quite entertaining.

You may wonder why this is in the chapter on Hypocrisy. That's because no matter how much we accuse them of being intolerant, in actuality we must be completely intolerant of anything related to conservative, Republican, Christian, Jewish or anti-socialist views. Just refuse to acknowledge that it is intolerant. We have mastered the art of the double-talking hypocrite. The Conservatives, on the other hand, are still held back by those pesky morals and trying to tell the truth. Since we don't have to worry about that, it's much easier for us to employ this tactic to undermine their credibility with the general public.

One of the most brilliant modern applications of hypocrisy is our use of Muslims to further our cause. The ridiculousness of this is almost incomprehensible. Islamic law and ideals do not generally align with our goals. However, they do support the destruction of The United States of America. This is enough common ground for us to build an alliance. Many Islamic countries will actually execute homosexuals, yet our uneducated masses will organize LGBT rallies supporting Islam!

This is so unbelievable that it vividly demonstrates the lack of education amongst our followers and clearly demonstrates how well they mindlessly follow orders. We scream tolerance, while our Muslim allies are anti-Semitic, anti-gay and anti-Christian! It's easy to rectify this discrepancy. We simply do not acknowledge the clearly racist, intolerant and extremist behavior of the radical Muslims, unless we can use it in some way to support one of our narratives. Muslims are gaining positions within the government at an impressive rate. Hamtramck, Michigan just elected an all-Muslim City council. We now even have Muslim operatives in the United States Congress actively working to destroy the country. An amazing aspect to this is that they are vocal about their destructive actions, and they still have the support of the liberal population! It doesn't hurt that they are elected from areas of the country that have high concentrations of Muslim immigrants. Many of these legal and illegal immigrants arrive here in the United States with preformed hatred of everything American.

The levels of hypocrisy are almost laughable, but helpful nonetheless. These immigrants leave their Muslim nations, stricken with poverty, oppression and religious intolerance. They move to the United States and immediately support the same policies and oppressive religious beliefs that they just escaped. In fact, they demand Americans respect these same beliefs as well! Clearly, we should treat these simpletons as a tool to help further the destruction of Christianity. Quite frankly, it's almost unbelievable how many Americans wholeheartedly support the advancement of Islam in the United States, just so that they can hold aloft the banner of being "tolerant", despite the fact that the radical Muslim movement would gladly snuff out the lives of every single non-Muslim in the country.

I will end this chapter with an awesome quote from Hillary Clinton from an interview on '60 Minutes'. Obviously, as good leftists, we often look to her for examples to follow, and after all, this is a chapter on hypocrisy: "The American people are tired of liars and people who pretend to be something they're not."13 - Hillary Clinton. She actually said that! That is amazing! Hypocrisy at its best, and she can do it with a straight face.

Chapter 5

Hate

"We can and must write in a language which sows among the masses hate, revulsion, and scorn toward those who disagree with us." – Lenin 14

Hate is certainly another one of our big guns. Like hypocrisy, it is woven into the very fabric of most of our policies, beliefs and actions. You must learn to absolutely HATE the Republicans, and especially the more conservative Republicans. We must HATE their ideas, their children, and their beliefs, essentially anything that they believe, do, or hold dear. Additionally, and more importantly, we must train hate into everyone that we can. Brainwash your children to hate conservatives. Spew hate at our followers, especially the young. Condition them into believing that this hatred in natural and necessary. Young people often want something to protest, they want to stand up against something.

Use this, exploit this to breed the hate that we need to rip this country apart. Former President Obama was a master of this technique. We can learn from his brilliant example. He was able to give a speech about tolerance and unity, while simultaneously sowing the seeds of hate and discord. It was a beautiful thing to watch, almost like art. Continue to foster this hate. Never allow healing between the two sides. Doing so, could undermine our objectives.

By fostering hate on our side, the self-righteous conservatives will fall right into the trap and hate us back. That's a good thing. By doing this, they are helping us keep the country divided. A divided country will be easier to conquer. Quite frankly, there really is nothing that anyone can do at this point to reunite the "United" States.

The chasm is so great, the left and right are so far apart, that all we really need to do is keep recruiting and the country should destroy itself within the next generation, two generations at most. As the country struggles, we will be able to take advantage of the disorder by providing a "solution". Of course, it will be a solution that benefits us. "In the midst of chaos, there is also opportunity."-Sun Tzu.40

Osama Bin Laden is rumored to have once said that "Americans have the watches, but we have the time." This is one of the many approaches that we share with radical Islamic terrorists. Bin Laden's approach was that if he didn't kill you, that's ok. His children would kill your children or his grandchildren would kill your grandchildren. Brilliant! If you look at the history of Far Left in this country, we've been working on advancing socialism and encouraging the eventual destruction of this nation for literally generations. Now, we are finally on the brink of success. (See Chapter 13, Playing the Long Game)

A very important aspect of our campaign of hate and destruction is the general hatred of law enforcement agencies and especially individual officers. This policy helps to support our overall goals in a few different ways. Firstly, the vast majority of police officers around the country are genuinely trying to reduce crime and get criminals off the street. This is unacceptable! This slows our march towards a societal breakdown.

We NEED high crime to help us instill a feeling of hopelessness in the general population. We NEED them to experience gun violence, so we can blame the guns. We NEED them to believe that there is no other alternative but to look to big government for help. These do-gooder cops are a huge obstacle to our advancement towards instability.

When law enforcement is ineffective, we and the common criminals can take advantage of that environment to do whatever we want. These cops want to hold everyone to the same standards. They don't understand that the laws of the commoner do not apply to the ranks of the liberal elite.

These agencies cannot be allowed to run around enforcing the law and investigating crimes without some checks and balances. The Liberal elites in this country have too much to lose if law enforcement looks too closely at our activities. We have a decades old tradition of tax evasion, pedophilia, bribery, money laundering and so much more. I could write an entire book on just how much we have stolen from charities. Free money! Conservatives LOVE to help the needy. They send the money, we steal it. It's a beautiful thing! www.clintonfoundation.org

With these things in mind, we must make every effort to protect ourselves. Once we've reestablished this country as a Socialist safe haven, we will no longer have to worry about hiding these activities. However, in the meantime, we must keep law enforcement agencies at a distance to protect ourselves. Of course, our Democratic allies in the House and Senate go to great lengths to assist us in this. After all, it's in their best interest as well since most of them are doing many of the same activities!

Let's get back to hating cops. Most conservatives support law enforcement. These short-sighted twits liken it to being patriotic and supporting the military! Donald Trump consistently showed his support again and again for law enforcement. Disgusting! We can leverage this perceived connection between law enforcement and Conservatives to help paint cops as the enemy to our followers.

In Chapter 3, we discussed taking advantage of violence between cops and minorities. However, these cops are getting smarter and harder to goad into a fight. We must be prepared to push violence on the cops if they aren't making mistakes for us to take advantage of.

This is already happening across the country. For example, in New York City (a gun free zone) we have examples of cops being ambushed and shot. This will help to frustrate the police and increase their likelihood of using violence against the citizens. This sets the stage for us to maximize on the potentially explosive scenario being created and drive the wedge deeper and deeper, thus setting the stage for yet more violence which leads to more hate. And hate is our friend.

With all this talk about hating cops, we can't forget the success stories where the cops have been muzzled and taken out of the equation. Let's look to places like Maryland and Washington State where the local Liberal mayors simply handicap the law enforcement so effectively that they are essentially unable to do their job. In more than one case they literally ordered the police to do nothing while our supporters looted and destroyed entire areas of the cities. It was a true success story.

There is another way to make the police incapable of performing their job, and the Democratic party has people already working on it.

Currently, the U.S. has something called "Qualified Immunity". In a nutshell, it protects various government officials (including police) from being directly sued as an individual for civil damages. As long as the officer didn't violate constitutional rights or clearly established laws, you can't sue that officer. Now

I'm not suggesting that we eliminate Qualified Immunity altogether because we can still use it to potentially protect our operatives in the current government. However, we should fight to remove the police from those who are protected by Qualified Immunity. Think about this: Imagine if you could sue a police officer for arresting you!

We could sue the cops into poverty. No law enforcement officers would be able to risk doing their jobs because they would all end up in court, fighting for their own livelihood. This effect would exponentially increase crime in the U.S. overnight. This would further fuel the hatred towards the police because the general population would feel as if this increase in crime was the police's fault. It was touched on earlier in this book; the higher the crime, the higher the hopelessness, and the easier it is to have big government sweep in and "save the day".

We have been so effective at sewing hate, that millions of our followers now blindly hate anything Republican, no matter what it is. Recently, it was a common joke is that if Donald Trump could have cured cancer, we could have made him look bad for putting oncologists out of work! That's pretty funny, and not entirely untrue. If you ask the average Democrat on the street if they liked

Donald Trump, almost every single one will declare their hatred for him and call him various names.

However, often times, they cannot name one single thing that he did during his presidency that they disagree with. They will usually just default to calling him a racist or compare him to Hitler, even though they don't know of one fact to support either of these claims.

This is a testament to the effectiveness of our campaign of hate. We have taught the ignorant masses to hate Republicans and Conservatives in general, and they do! They really do! We must continue this onslaught of teaching hatred. This is not a new technique.

Once again, we can look to the great Joseph Goebbels, who once said that "Propaganda must facilitate the displacement of aggression by specifying the targets for hatred".15 The uneducated masses that form the majority of our ranks must be given direction. They must be given a target. They must be told what to hate, and that responsibility falls to us, the Liberal Elite, to direct that hate and harness it.

Not every voter has the time or desire to pay attention to politics. This is great for us too. We don't even have to convince this group to agree with our policies. Just convince them that someone is an evil, racist, fascist, sexist or elitist and they will hate him and vote against him. Mission accomplished. Of note, this description actually accurately describes many Democrats.

Do not let the uneducated be aware of the truth about our Democratic candidates or elected officials and deflect any bad press towards the other side. If anyone tries to point out the disgraceful (and sometimes illegal) activities of our Democratic members, just deny everything, claim that it was actually the Republicans who were acting illegally and act outraged that they would even suggest that our upstanding members could be capable of such a thing. That leads us into our next chapter...

Chapter 6

Outrage and the Victim Mentality

As liberals, we can be outraged at anything and everything. This trick is useful for whipping our followers up into a frenzy. Typically, the average uneducated young person will not know when to be upset. They will either walk around happy and oblivious, or they will just act angry at everything. As leaders, we must inform the masses when they should be outraged. Again, we can use this as we see fit. We must tell them to be outraged at essentially anything the Republicans do. Additionally, we can use this as a distraction to call attention away from things that we do not want to be in the limelight.

For example, let's say that we have a Democratic Senator that is being investigated for sexual misconduct, stealing campaign funds or using official government transportation to visit his mistress, all very realistic scenarios. We can simply instruct a group of young, loud believers to be "outraged" at something that some random Republican has done. Then we call up the main stream media and put these outraged, outspoken activists on television. The news organizations that are blatantly supporting us will focus on our newly invented "problem" and will barely cover the other story, or ignore it altogether.

To strengthen the ploy, we can add in some "victims" that we create. Not only are these young people outraged, but they have been viciously targeted by "(Fill in whoever or whatever we want right here)"! And since we are inventing both the outrage and the victim situation, we can use whatever we want to achieve our goal. Facts, truth or actual events are not necessarily required. However, the puppets that we use need to be convincing. Since the liberal masses seldom do any actual research, these "victims" just need to be told that an atrocity has been committed against them and they should be outraged!

Obviously, this method would not work if we didn't have the media outlets in our corner. However, that's not a problem. They literally don't even try to hide it any more. Luckily, most Americans are oblivious to what is going on around them, so they don't even notice. That's part of the beauty of being a liberal.

Since we don't have any real morals, it makes it easy to take advantage of anyone and everyone who is not diligent enough to educate themselves! They just simply turn on the same station that they have always listened to and we can pour our propaganda right into their brains. The system is not quite as good as the one enjoyed in North Korea, but it's not bad considering the whole "freedom of speech" obstacle that we have to negotiate here in the U.S.

Fortunately for us, the 1st Amendment provides us freedom of the press, but does not put any requirements on reporting truthfully! At one point, Donald Trump had gained some traction against us, fighting back with his "Fake News" narrative. However, the term has actually become so over-used that it has essentially lost its effectiveness.

The liberal media puts so many intentionally misleading news stories out there, that those on the right struggle to counter every single one. However, because they are constantly pointing out our lies and yelling "Fake News", it actually weakens the effectiveness of the claim because everyone constantly hears it. The people start to get accustomed to it and the claims simply become white noise in an already overactive news cycle. So, we just need to keep driving forward with our manipulation of the American public on a massive scale and it will overwhelm those who are trying to protect the people from our storyline.

Fidel Castro once said: "The first thing dictators do is finish free press, to establish censorship. There is no doubt that a free press is the first enemy of dictatorship."16 Clearly, we can learn a lot from the techniques of Fidel Castro. That is one of the reasons that he is held in such high regard by our uneducated followers. However, in this case I have to point out that it is not just important to finish free press. We must continue to make it appear that the free press still exists and use that press as a conduit to keep our flow of misinformation and subversion pumping into the minds of the public. We can then leverage our use of outrage against any source of news that does not support our point of view.

Another way that we can use outrage to advance our plot is to get the most out of every tragedy that we can, and paint ourselves or our supporters as "victims". One of our "go-to" actions is to pounce on any kind of firearms-related incident to try and advance our anti-gun policies. We'll explore this more in Chapter 10 (Be anti-gun). However, what is important is to utilize the tragedy while it is still headline news. Exploit as many crying children, grieving mothers, and self-righteous teenage activists as possible.

Plus, bring in our pseudo-clergymen to fan the flames. Our "reverends" may actually be more corrupt than our politicians (impressive, I know), but they will still stand on their sanctimonious pulpits and point accusatory fingers at the "pro-gun" Republicans (and the masses in general) and people will listen to them, just because of that religious title! Of course, this only works when our puppets are believable, so our religious representatives must be adept liars as well.

However, this is not a problem since they've been lying for so long that they can do it with a straight face and make it sound like they are simply looking out for the flock! This brilliant network of corrupt actors pretending to be Christians are capable of doing a tremendous amount of damage. This is strengthened by the fact that many of them are not only "clergy", but they are black clergy! So, if anyone disagrees with them, we can easily add "racism" to the mix! (See Chapter 3, Racism and Other Useful Discriminatory Practices)

To understand the genius behind this group, you must keep in mind that not all Democratic voters would be on board with our deception. Many Democratic voters are actually trying to be good Christians, good Americans and good people in general. We must keep these people voting Democrat, and we can't do that if they realize that we stand against all those things. That's where our lying, deceptive "reverends" come into play. They must keep these good people believing that liberalism is a good thing. If these good people realize the truth, we'll surely lose their vote to the Republicans. We'll talk more about this technique in Chapter 12, Misdirection and Outright Lies.

Let's continue with our discussion on how to best take advantage of tragedies. While the family, community or country is still hurting, we need to point out that no matter what the tragedy is, it was obviously created or facilitated by conservative policies.

We then must scream that the only possible answer is to immediately demand a vote on new legislation to protect our country and our children! It doesn't matter if the new laws are actually helpful. As a matter of fact, we typically know that they will have absolutely no effect on crime. However, what is important is that the new laws MUST advance our agenda. Restrictive laws are often passed during times of turmoil due to emotional voting. Oftentimes the citizens are not even asking for the new laws, but our brilliant, manipulative operatives in Congress will capitalize on the moment to attempt to push through a piece of legislation that "can't wait" to be voted on.

The public will get behind the new knee-jerk law and the citizens will cry out for us to take their rights away! This plays right into our hands. This is exactly the kind of voting we need to take advantage of. Use this time to call the new restrictive laws "Common Sense Legislation", because who can argue with using common sense, right? As a backup plan, if no one is protesting or seeking the legislation that we want to advance, we'll just inform some of our "activists" that they are now "outraged" and they need to get out on the street ASAP! The part that often escapes the news is that this "new" legislation is being presented immediately following an incident and may be dozens, or even hundreds of pages long.

How did that proposed bill get produced seemingly overnight? It didn't. Luckily for us, our Democratic protectors in the government keep many "wish list" bills prepared and ready to go. They are just waiting for the appropriate disaster or death to throw it into the mix. Additionally, many other completely unrelated items will be conveniently woven into the fabric of the multi-page document. So, we will be pushing a certain subject (for example, gun control), but in actuality, buried deep in the intentionally vague and confusing verbiage is additional legislation doing something completely unrelated to the supposed intent of the bill (for example, funding overseas abortions or increasing emission restrictions on automobiles). And don't think that our brilliant leaders in Washington only use that trick on the "emergency, common sense" legislation. Slipping our wish list of legislation into every bill has become the standard. They now do it to essentially every single piece of legislation that is produced.

Add to that the practice of naming the bill something positive like "The NY SAFE Act", or using a victim's name to invoke pity or public support and this further increases our likelihood of success. We also take advantage of the Republicans' desire to pass their own bills. We can agree to support a Republican bill, only IF we get to add in our own piece of poison. Often times, the Republicans are so focused on getting their piece of legislation pushed through that they will not even give us much pushback when we add OUR agenda to THEIR law! So even when they are "winning", we are still advancing our overall agenda, and we look reasonable for doing so!

Unfortunately, sometimes we have to wait too long between tragedies, and we need something to be outraged at. We can still use the "Outrage" tactic. As was mentioned at the beginning of this chapter, we can simply wait for the Republicans to do literally anything and feign outrage! Then, we must pursue it with fervor, as if what they did was absolutely unbelievable! If our agenda requires an additional boost, we have some insanely wealthy benefactors to help fund these efforts. We have money coming from Americans (especially New York and California), Hungarian-Americans, Russians,

Chinese, you name it. The whole world wants the United States of America knocked off of its pedestal, and we now have the financial backing to do it. Trust me, when we need a tragic crisis to be created, it can be done. It's easier to be outraged when you are getting paid to do so.

Especially if this involves organizing some type of protest. Keep in mind that it is easier to motivate the poor or lazy with promises of "equality" when you give them something. This serves two purposes. Initially, it encourages them to get up off the couch or out of their parent's basement with the promise of money or reward. Secondly, we are engineering their thought processes to believe that this cause is "right".

Young people are idealistic, which makes them easier to control, and therefore it is easier to instill outrage in them. When we immerse them with others who have been similarly manipulated, this outrage grows and strengthens the mindset in the group. It's simple mob mentality and it works like a charm. In the past we have even rented busses to ship in our additional hired protesters to bolster our numbers and add more "victims" to the mix. This larger crowd emboldens our pawns and makes them feel untouchable. The larger the crowd, the more you feel like your actions will not have repercussions.

Once we have the created a large enough crowd, then it's time to insert a loud-mouthed catalyst into this scenario and get the crowd all fired up. This is a good time to use one of those "celebrities" that we talked about earlier in the book. This same person can be charged with keeping the group on task in accordance with our script. We must make sure the group is putting on a good show for the media. The media will help us out as much as they can by manipulating camera angles or "miscalculating" the number of people in the crowd to make out numbers look better. However, we have to do our part as well. We must ensure that we inform everyone of what they are outraged by and encourage them to be as loud and energetic as possible to highlight how "passionate" they are about the subject!

To understand the strength of manufactured outrage, you must appreciate that it can be inserted into nearly any scenario or argument to strengthen your position. This is effective in a face-to-face argument as well as interviews. However, we really see the power of this tool when it is utilized in a crowd setting. Incredulous outrage by a motivated and inspired speaker is a quick way to work a crowd into a frenzy. You can steer the attitude of a crowd or rally and drive them like cattle towards the result that you are attempting to achieve. You can use it to fuel the mob mentality. You can use it to encourage behavior. You can plant the idea in their minds that they are the victim here.

They were intentionally targeted and they should feel as if they've been victimized, violated! But most importantly, you can use this scenario to control others. The masses need guidance to ensure that, at all times, they are being efficiently utilized to achieve the party goals.

Chapter 7

Smug Intellectualism

Smug intellectualism has proven to be particularly useful when used in conjunction with our media partners. People like to have smart leaders. It makes them feel safe and protected, especially when they make no actual effort to maintain their own safety or protection. However, obviously many of our leaders (elected or otherwise) are not exactly intellectual powerhouses. So how do we counter this? Fake it! Since nearly every news outlet only supports our liberal narrative, we can manipulate the conversation in various ways to make our side appear more intelligent and believable and to make the conservatives appear uninformed, uneducated or simple minded.

However, this is a double-edged sword and we must be careful. If we allow the conservatives to engage us on equal ground with equal resources, they could make us look foolish or expose our lies. Therefore, anytime we have a televised "discussion" make sure that we stack the deck dramatically in our favor. Here is some helpful guidance for our main stream media lackeys:

First of all, make sure that the liberal representative has all of the questions ahead of time and has time to prepare articulate answers that are in accordance with the party guidance at the time. (I say "at the time" since our positions can change at any moment, we have to make sure that we aren't using last week's storyline.) Do not let the conservatives have any information beforehand. We've used this trick successfully in everything from town hall meetings all the way up to presidential debates.

If you ask the question to our side first, make sure that you allow our pundit plenty of time to answer. Then, allow the other side to answer. However, keep the camera on our "expert" most of the time that the conservative is answering. With this simple maneuver, we can still communicate with the audience, even while the conservative is talking. Our representative can shake his head, roll his eyes and laugh at the other person while the other person is talking.

This will delegitimize the answer in the eyes of many people, even if the conservative's answer was accurate. This method was used so effectively in the 2012 vice-presidential debate, that after the debate, even the conservative station said that then Vice President Biden had done better than Congressman Ryan.

They essentially agreed that Vice President Biden had won, albeit narrowly, the debate. However, if you were to have read a transcript of the debate, the Republican, Congressman Ryan, often gave much better answers. It didn't matter. We had a liberal moderator and it was covered in such a way that it benefitted our side. Everything from facial expressions to camera angles were used to discreetly influence the viewers and delegitimize Congressman Ryan's answers, and it was done in a manner that the majority of the public did not even realize that they were being manipulated.

Of course, we went on to win the election as well. It may have only been a small part, but that's the way that we are going to take this country, one little piece at a time. It's death by a thousand small cuts.

Another beneficial technique when having "debates" on your news programs is to follow any conservative answer with a long-winded response from one of our "experts". It doesn't matter if our mouthpiece has any actual qualifications or experience, it just matters that they speak last and with believable authority.

These techniques of manipulation are not only beneficial for influencing conversations in the media, but these same methods should be employed simply to guide day to day conversations. This commitment will ensure that we are consistently reinforcing our agenda with our followers and continually attempting to convert nonbelievers. Additionally, always remember that if the truth is not helpful, avoid it and push the party agenda. (See Chapter 12, Misdirection and Outright lies.) I think the value of these techniques was very well indicated by Joseph Goebbels, who was reported to have said, "Think of the press as a great keyboard on which the government can play."[17]

A key factor to using Smug Intellectualism effectively is simply believing in what you are saying. Back in Chapter One, I mentioned that you do not need actual facts or historical data. While that is true, whatever information or data that you do use, should still sound believable and you must buy into it as well. Or at least you must appear to believe in it. Always assume an air of superiority and treat your opponents as if they are uneducated and uninformed. In Chapter 12, Misdirection and Outright Lies, there are several techniques that you can use to reinforce your position and ensure that you are maintaining the appearance of being in control of the conversation.

The end result of this smug intellectualism will demoralize your opponent as well as help influence anyone observing. You will appear to be more educated, more conscientious, and more confident. Using this technique while simultaneously establishing your moral superiority is a great way to win nearly any argument or debate. If this still doesn't work, call them a racist.

Chapter 8

Embrace Islam

"Islam is the fastest-growing religion in America, a guide and pillar of stability for many of our people..."~Hillary Clinton, Los Angeles Times, May 31st, 1996[18]

The embracing of Islam by the left is confounding to the conservatives. They simply can't understand why any Americans, even Liberals, would willfully join forces with a group of people that are actively seeking the destruction of the country. It's actually quite simple. However, first, it is important to understand that the mainstream liberal population is so wrapped up in ensuring "equal treatment" of everyone, that they will do nearly anything to avoid appearing racist, sexist or biased against a religion.

This includes the proclamation of tolerance towards those that wish to do America harm. So that helps to explain one reason why we must embrace Islam. We must maintain the appearance that we care about everyone equally, when in reality, we are just using these people as we would use any other pawn. (See Chapter 4, Hypocrisy)

Secondly, the advancement of Islam supports our overall goal of eroding the moral norms of the past. You should notice this as a consistent theme throughout this writing. Essentially, we are going to support anything that works to undermine the Christian ideals or traditional moral fabric of the United States. If you look at the guidelines of Sharia law, they are opposed to nearly every aspect of a free society. That's great! Any additional influence that helps destroy the status quo within the country can be used as a springboard for advancing our destruction of the country. This de facto destruction is, of course, merely a stepping stone on the path to rebuilding the country under a true Socialist model. This new society will need "leadership" (a ruling class) and that is where we, as the liberal elite, will be able to take our rightful place as rulers of the peasants.

Now you must understand that we don't actually support Islam taking over the U.S. That would be counterproductive to our plan. So, we must use this large group of people just like we use any other disposable tool. Drive them towards something that we want to influence, use them any way possible and then throw them away like garbage.

Chapter 9

LGBT

Our relationship with the LGBT+ community was born out of convenience. Generally speaking, most Christians will have more in common with the conservative movement. Additionally, most Christian organizations still cling to the traditional teachings of the bible, which do not support homosexuality (although we are gaining ground in this area). Therefore, by default, the beliefs and ideals of the LGBT community typically are incompatible with the beliefs of much of the conservative population. Regardless of our beliefs on the subject, we can seize this opportunity to leverage the LGBT groups to our side at the ballot box. Just like the Muslims, this group should be viewed as a disposable asset that may be exploited for votes.

Additionally, a large portion of our heterosexual supporters (voters) want to prove how tolerant they are of alternative lifestyles. In order for them to prove to others how "tolerant" and therefore "liberal" they are, they will speak out in support of anything LGBT, no matter how outrageous or deviant. In order to keep these single-issue voters happy and voting in our corner, we can simply pander to these various groups. As a liberal elite, it is our responsibility to manipulate these pawns and prey upon their blind determination to look tolerant.

At its core, the LGBT agenda supports our continuing theme of being generally destructive to anything reminiscent of the old America. The LGBT community continues to add additional "alternative" lifestyles to their ranks. For example, in chapter one, we mentioned the reclassification of pedophilia as a sexual preference.

This should be whole heartedly supported. We have a couple different approaches that we may utilize to support this bold advancement. First, we can simply force the issue that the attraction to children is nothing more than another acceptable sexual orientation and that anyone not embracing this is being intolerant. An alternate approach, with potentially more long reaching affect, may be to have the adult simply "identify" as a child. For instance, suppose we have a forty-something male who is sexually attracted to ten-year-old boys. This is helpful to us as liberals, since it supports the destruction of the old school moral fabric of Christian America.

As mentioned in earlier chapters, a good liberal can't be distracted by the damage being done to the children. You must keep in mind that there are plenty of children in America and if we, as liberals, must sacrifice their mental or physical health to advance the deconstruction of the old national moral code, then do so emphatically. We should support this man's insistence that he is merely a victim of being born in the wrong body and at the wrong time and he is actually a ten-year-old girl (or he can "identify" as a ten-year-old girl). Therefore, his attraction to ten-year-old boys should be viewed as completely natural. (Reference Chapter 1, Understanding the Brilliance of Liberalism)

This book is not the place to address the exceptionally high suicide rate in the LGBT community, because it is not important to us.19 Just as with minorities, we liberals don't have to actually care about the LGBT community. We just need to leverage them as a tool in our march to power. However, we can take advantage of the comparatively high amount of mental illness in the group.

The mentally ill, just like the mentally incompetent can be manipulated more easily into believing our propaganda. Take advantage of their weaknesses. Seize upon their desires for acceptance. Give them a group that welcomes them into the ranks. We can use forward thinking ideas such as those presented by Dr. Elizabeth Riley, from Australia, who stated in an interview with 60 Minutes, Extra Minutes that "Until society can get that some boys are born with vaginas and some girls are born with penises, we're always going to have this problem about how children see themselves and what they have to do in order to be accepted."37

Rather than acknowledge that an individual might actually need mental health assistance, just celebrate the illness and call them heroic. If anyone on the other side of the aisle does not support the stance that a man can have a vagina or that a woman can have a penis, call them a bigot and a homophobe and discredit them with our version of science. You can also call them a racist, just for good measure.

The bottom line is that in our advancement towards the "new" United States, we must embrace and support anything that tears down the "old" United States. You can't build a house where a house is already standing. You must first tear down the old house to allow the new one to take its place. This is the mindset that we are embracing. We will use whatever tool is required. If that tool happens to be a homosexual, no problem. If that tool is a bunch of mentally ill sexual deviants, still no problem, as long as they vote Democrat.

Chapter 10

Be Anti-Gun

This is one of the hottest subjects in the modern left vs right debates. In fact, it could be argued by some that this is one of the most significant debates in the entire history of the country. There is no room for compromise, understanding or debate. When it comes to the subject of firearms, we must band together and support any and every effort to restrict, deny, confiscate or regulate firearms ownership by the private citizen.

We will be consistently steadfast in our belief that there is no reasonable excuse for the average American citizen to own these weapons of war which have no other intended design but to kill. At this point, you may be asking "why?" The answer is very straight forward and rooted in the history of Socialism and Communism. In order for us to emplace a totalitarian socialist regime, we MUST remove the people's ability to fight back. It's Tyranny 101 and has been proven by many of the greats over the years: Hitler, Lenin, Stalin, Mao Zedong, Chavez.

Now, in order to support this point of view, it will be necessary to ignore some facts and historical examples. As I have pointed out in earlier chapters, facts, truth or even logic are not necessary to mount a feasible defense of our positions. I'm going to help you understand how to fight these right-wing nut cases and their pro-gun arguments.

The most common argument is the statement that the right to have guns is simply guaranteed by the constitution. There is more than one way to counter this argument. You can point out that the founding fathers had no concept that the American public would be able to buy "Assault Rifles" 200 years in the future and therefore, the basic right should now be reviewed or revoked. Now, if you do any basic research on the subject, you may already know that the AR-15 and the AK-47 that are available for civilian purchase are actually different from actual assault rifles or machine guns.

However, research or a basic knowledge of firearms is unnecessary and a waste of time, so don't even acknowledge the difference. Just focus on the fact that they look like military weapons and just lump them all together under the moniker of "weapons of war" or "assault rifle". Why would anyone possibly want to own a weapon of war, unless they intended to murder people? Ignore the fact that millions of these guns are owned in the United States and are never used for anything illegal. Just focus on the rare occasion that one can be linked to a crime.

The right wing "sportsmen" will try to point out that the guns are used for hunting, recreational shooting, or home defense purposes. Apply a liberal amount of smug intellectualism and point out that they are poorly suited for any of these applications and these purposes are just a ruse to cover up the actual intent of using these guns for mass shootings later. There is no data to support this claim of course, so you must be steadfast in your belief. You can also make up any statistics that you need to support your stance. (See Chapter 12, Misdirection and Outright Lies)

This is also a great time to imply that anyone with an assault rifle must be a lunatic conspiracy theorist. This has nothing to do with them owning a gun, but it helps to paint them in the light of an unstable "wacko", therefore destroying any credibility of their arguments. This sets you up to say condescending remarks like "That's exactly what a conspiracy theorist would say." It doesn't matter if it has any bearing on the actual argument. You can use this tool to dismiss the enemy's arguments and simultaneously frustrate the conservative.

If they try to point out the times that guns have been used to prevent crime or to protect innocents, energetically point out that that is the job of the police. Point out that civilians carrying guns are just sociopaths looking for an excuse to kill people and get away with it. Don't get this confused with actually supporting the police, which we do not do. This is just an excuse for why private citizens don't need guns. (See Chapter 4, Hypocrisy)

Keep in mind that the vast majority of the Police in this country are our enemies. We are not actually showing any support or confidence in law enforcement, we are just using them as part of our hypocritical argument to support why private citizens do not need guns. If you need more guidance on how to properly hate the police, see Chapter 5, Hate.

The gun-rights supporters will try to point out that the Founding Fathers wanted us to be able to defend ourselves against tyranny. Laugh in their faces. Point out that the government is much too strong to stand up against. Tell them that that argument is ridiculous and that no one would dare stand up against the U.S. government. President Joe Biden even reinforced this on June 23rd, 2021 in remarks at the White House: "If you wanted or if you think you need to have weapons to take on the government, you need F-15s and maybe some nuclear weapons. The point is that there has always been the ability to limit — rationally limit the type of weapon that can be owned and who can own it."21

The president went on to eloquently say: "The Second Amendment, from the day it was passed, limited the type of people who could own a gun and what type of weapon you could own. You couldn't buy a cannon. Those who say the 'blood of patriots,' you know, and all the stuff about how we're going to have to move against the government. Well, the tree of liberty is not watered with the blood of patriots."21

Once again, there is no need to research the accuracy of his statement. Don't check to see if it's true. If you are already aware that the Second Amendment did not limit the type of people who could buy a gun, or if you already know that a private citizen could, in fact, purchase a cannon back then, just ignore the facts and support our leader and the party stance.

Besides, as long as we are in charge, the government is always "looking out for our best interest." Stick with this general stance and do not waiver in your insistence that guns are bad, dangerous, unnecessary, or whatever else you can come up with to delegitimize their arguments.

We, of course, know the truth. In order for us to emplace a true totalitarianism regime, we will have to disarm the population. A wonderful example was the techniques used by the great Joseph Stalin in the last century. By the time Stalin stepped into power, the Bolsheviks had all but disarmed the Russian people as a whole.

Stalin was able to use political force, demonstrated ruthless killings and the intimidation of a secret police to silence those who disagreed with his politics. Some may try to point out that the collective policies and other factors at the time resulted in the death of an estimated 20 million people under Stalin's watchful eye. Others may try to lump all of the deaths under Communist rule into one big pile.

However, no one really knows how many people died under the hand of Communism. In the 20th Century alone, estimates range from 60 million to as high as 150 million. However, these numbers highlight the effectiveness of disarming the people. Let's focus on the collective good that was accomplished with those deaths. First and foremost, they led to the ruling class being able to live a life of plenty and govern more effectively.

Additionally, the labor provided by these political dissidents in the political labor camps helped improve the infrastructure and economy of the nation. Finally, these deaths helped reduced the need for food in the poverty-stricken regions and therefore lessened the effects of famine and shortages. These positive results could have been greatly handicapped by the people if the general population had been an armed citizenry. Luckily, the people were not able to take part in the illegal activity of fighting back against the government. Likewise, we don't want the American public to be able to defend themselves either.

Unfortunately, right now, we still have a long way to go to get the guns out of the hands of the law-abiding public. I say the law-abiding public because obviously we are not concerned with disarming the criminals. The illegal aliens, gangs, terrorists, organized crime groups or common street thugs don't obey the gun laws anyhow, so really when we pass gun laws, they are obviously just meant to affect the law-abiding citizenry. To anyone who looks critically at our proposed gun laws, it will be obvious that we are not trying to make America safer. We are literally simply trying to disarm the people. However, we can use false statistics and simply lie about whatever we need to in order to support our claims of the opposite. For example, during the presidential debates of 2020, then candidate Joe Biden claimed that 150 million people had been killed since 2007 by guns.22

That would have been nearly half of the United States population. Clearly, that was not true. However, it's yet another great example of how we can simply invent whatever statistic we need in order to support our claim. Some may claim that this was just another of Mr. Biden's dementia-induced missteps. Regardless, it's another example of how we can get away with saying whatever we want, with no repercussions to our deceit. (See Chapter 12, Misdirection and Outright Lies)

You need to understand that none of these arguments are not intended to sway the hard-core gun fanatics. You are never going to convince these right-wing gun supporters to change their ways. Your arguments should be used to influence the uninformed public and to galvanize our other supporters. The public must support, even demand additional gun control legislation.

That is how we will win the fight. We are probably never going to be able to go door to door and confiscate guns like they did in Russia. Instead, we will legislate them out of the hands of law-abiding citizens. We must emplace registration, fees, licensing, restrictions or anything that makes it more difficult and expensive to buy, own, shoot or carry guns.

Recently, Virginia has been doing just that. They are passing law after law restricting firearms and ammunition in every way possible. The people of the state are rising up, speaking out and making their voices heard that they do not want the legislation. Luckily, we have a bought and paid for Democratic governor and Democratic control in both houses that don't care what the people want. They are simply staying focused on the advancement of the anti-gun agenda of the party. This is great! It's just like having a little slice of California on the east coast.

Now, a side note to all this talk about getting rid of guns: Don't worry about yourself. As a liberal elite and a member of the ruling class, you will be afforded armed protection because your life is worth more than the lives of the proletariat. A great example of this is to simply look at all the current Democratic legislators leading the charge against guns in the country. Many maintain armed guards any time they want. (See Chapter 4, Hypocrisy)

Chapter 11

Violence

I need to start off this chapter by saying that violence is NEVER the answer! At least that is our official stance and anytime that the conservatives or other right-wing entities use violence, we should condemn it in the strongest language possible. Be outraged! Insult their intelligence and accuse them of being barbarians or animals!

Now that we have gotten that out of the way, let's look at how we can use violence to get our way:

I've intentionally placed this chapter following the chapter on Being Anti-gun to highlight our effective use of hypocrisy. Socialists, Communists and totalitarian regimes in general have always been very effective at utilizing violence to influence and shape the political landscape in our favor. We have plenty of successful examples to draw from in the past to show that the use of violence is not only helpful, but likely even necessary to the Socialist agenda.

This precision application of violence has already started to show its usefulness here in the United States. Earlier, I mentioned the Antifa movement. We want to always bill the Antifa groups as non-violent. However, that's clearly a lie. Our Antifa operatives must be ready to commit violence at any time and at any place where it might benefit us. We can wield them as our terrorism arm. Now, you may recoil from the use of that word, "terrorism", but let's look at it from a practical standpoint.

ter·ror·ism
/ˈterəˌrizəm/
noun
1.   the unlawful use of violence and intimidation, especially against civilians, in the pursuit of political aims.23

That's actually EXACTLY what we are doing! Obviously, we aren't going to call our activities terrorism, so we'll use less accurate, but more acceptable words such as "activism", "protest", "rally", or even "parade".   However, we definitely want our Antifa comrades to terrorize and intimidate anyone that we can bully into agreeing with us, or at the very least scare them away from opposing us. Remember: "Terrorism is the best political weapon for nothing drives people harder than a fear of sudden death." – Adolph Hitler24
While we are committing these acts of terrorism, you must constantly deny that it is terrorism.   In fact, roll your eyes, be dismissive and call the NRA or Christians or any other right wing group terrorists to help deflect from the truth.   We all know that it is, by definition, terrorism.   However, we must continue the non-stop propaganda assault on the uneducated masses to redirect any insinuation of wrong doing to those who are trying to expose us!   We'll talk more about this in Chapter 12, Misdirection and Outright Lies.
The tactics being utilized have been effective all over the world for centuries: masks or anonymity, the threat of violence, intimidation, massing groups of people to

give the appearance of strength, and of course actual violence.

By design, Antifa (or similar groups) will need to be made up by mostly young people. Young, uneducated, idealistic people will be easier to brainwash, manipulate and manage. It's really ironic that some of the best recruits are young people that actually want the best for the country, or even the world. Luckily for us, they are so idealistic and enthusiastic that when we tell them that Socialism means equality, they simply jump in with both feet to support this effort. After all, how could equality be bad?! They seldom ever take the time to look at all the historical examples of what Socialism or Communism actually is! You must be vigilant to always maintain this deception with these young recruits and keep up the blatant lie that everyone will be treated equally.

You need to understand that none of these arguments are intended to sway the hard-core gun fanatics. You are never going to convince these right-wing gun supporters to change their ways. Your arguments should be used to influence the uninformed public and to galvanize our other supporters. The public must support, even demand additional gun control legislation.

Luckily, we have liberal supporters in various government positions that will blatantly support us and facilitate our criminal activity. We have mayors and other political allies that will work with us to limit the interaction of the police and provide us with political and legal cover for our destructive, terroristic activities. Our political operatives in Maryland, California and Washington State have already proven to be effective in doing this and we have been gaining supporters in all three locations as a result.

Keep in mind that our violence, terrorism and intimidation does not have to be limited to just our Antifa pawns. Obviously, this dimwitted group is an easy weapon to throw at things. However, they are also quite public and need more than a bit of supervision to keep them pointed in the right direction. After all, this group of misguided simpletons is not exactly known for their mental gymnastics. This is the tool we use when we need to impart blunt force trauma into the political arena. However, sometimes we will want a more surgical application of violence or the threat of violence. Therefore, we must be able to diversify our tools.

We should never pass up an opportunity to use individuals or smaller groups to harass and interfere with the lives of conservatives and Republican politicians. Organize groups to harass them in public places such as coffee shops, restaurants, churches, or anywhere else that we can generally disrupt their lives. Take advantage of the mentally unstable to encourage them to do the same. However, do so in a manner that they don't realize that they are being manipulated. Get them whipped up into a frenzy and point them at a potential target.

If you have planted enough hate, misdirection and lies in their heads, they will hopefully escalate into violence that will serve our purposes, while giving us the plausible deniability to say that we "never saw it coming". If they happen to use firearms in their attacks, then that benefits us as well because we can use the attack as a springboard to launch additional attacks on the ability of law-abiding citizens to own guns. (Don't forget to be "appalled" by the violence and the use of these "weapons of war".)

As I addressed in Chapter 3, our allies may get hurt as well. Keep in mind, that as a Liberal Elite, you must not be concerned or dissuaded by the sacrifices of our pawns. We must have foot soldiers in this war and foot soldiers will be lost. They may be detained, injured or killed, but obviously, none of that is actually important to us. Just capitalize on the situation to further our cause. You may need to pretend that you care about their personal losses in order to best take advantage of it. Try to be believable, but never lose focus that in our true Socialist society, the ruling class will not actually mix with these working-class drones.

Chapter 12

Misdirection and Outright Lies

"It is not the truth that matters, but victory."
– Adolph Hitler25

Outright lies has always been an obvious tool used by Communists, Socialists, Liberals and Democrats throughout history. The effectiveness of this tool cannot be overstated. It is used almost constantly in nearly every aspect of dealing with the public, the right-wing enemy and of course when manipulating our mass of followers. You must not be afraid to tell complete and total lies with a straight face if it supports our efforts. "The whole secret lies in confusing the enemy, so that he cannot fathom our real intent."-Sun Tzu.40

Adolph Hitler was once quoted as saying "If you tell a big enough lie and tell it frequently enough, it will be believed."26 It has been speculated that this quote was Hitler's effort to reinforce one of the principal ideas of his propagandist, Joseph Goebbels who taught that "If you repeat a lie often enough, people will believe it, and you will even come to believe it yourself."27

He reinforced this idea with this statement: "A lie told once remains a lie but a lie told a thousand times becomes the truth."27 We must constantly and consistently push our agenda. We have been consistently successful in creating a new "truth", a new "normal" by simply repeating our lies over and over. With the modern connected society, we can accomplish a thousand lies in a single day. We must set our sights even higher and our lies will continue to be accepted as fact. Look at global warming, critical race theory, the use of the term "assault rifle". The list goes on and on. The key is to be persistent and repetitive.

This is a chapter on lying and how to use lying to our advantage, so let's look back at some famous examples in recent years: "I did not have sexual relations with that woman, Miss Lewinsky." ~President Bill Clinton28

"If you like your health care plan, you'll be able to keep your health care plan." ~President Barrack -Obama29 Now these two examples may actually be a little humorous, but I've chosen these specific examples because they are such blatant examples that they perfectly highlight the point that it genuinely doesn't matter what lies we say. It only matters that we repeat them often and emphatically!

Everyone in the country knew exactly what was going on with President Clinton and Monica Lewinsky. Yet, he stood in front of the camera, with Hillary Clinton by his side and made that claim to overwhelming applause from his supporters! The situation was so ludicrous that it is beyond laughable, and yet he stood there, straight-faced and delivered that famous line. This is not the only example to highlight the fact that the truth is inconsequential. However, this small book certainly is not the place to try to list the volumes of public lies made by Democrats to the American public. This is just to highlight the point that there is no need to concern yourself with the truth when advancing our movement.

President Clinton gave us a lot to work with in this chapter on Misdirection and Outright Lies. However, one quote from him almost found a place into two different chapter, as it highlights both lies and hypocrisy. "The road to tyranny, we must remember, begins with the destruction of the truth." ~ Bill Clinton30

Obviously, the quote was presented as if he were advocating against the destruction of truth. However, if we look at his history of "truthfulness", we can easily interpret that he was actually giving us a piece of the roadmap to power. We must control the narrative; we must consistently destroy any information that can be used against us.

As a group, we liberals have become masters of lies and deception. Take advantage of this fact to continue to spread deception, hate, lies and misdirection at every opportunity. As Liberals, we often look to the past for ideas, techniques and methods used to control the masses. The manipulation of people has not changed in eons. All that has changed is the delivery method. Maintain your lies, do not back down and no matter how ridiculous the claim is, just be adamant. You will be surprised at how many people will fall for this and even begin repeating your lies as their own new "truth".

A convincing method is to quote falsified statistics in a convincing manner. For example: "According to a recent three-year study by the University of New Jersey, 37% of gun owners have contemplated using their firearms for criminal purposes." I just made that up. There is no University of New Jersey. However, by including the name of an official sounding university and making the numbers high, but believable, you can present this deception as an irrefutable "fact".

The person that you are speaking to will not be able to mount an argument against it because they are not familiar with the study (since it never actually happened). Of course, you can use real universities or government agencies in your lie as well. "According to a recent study release by the CDC..." or "According to FBI crime statistics for 2016-2019..." or "UCLA just completed a multimillion-dollar, 8-year study of...". The more specific you are, the more believable your lie. A common joke is that 48% of all statistics are made up on the spot. Of course, that's a made-up number that is part of the joke. However, it highlights the actual technique that can be used as part of our deception.

For now, the first amendment protects the freedom of speech, but it places no requirements on that speech being truthful. The first amendment also protects the freedom of the press. Likewise, nothing says that the news has to be truthful or accurate. Liberals have been able to weaponize this fact and perfected the art of the doubletalk to leverage it in our favor.

Our liberal friends in the media will lie for us without giving it a second thought. Once again, we can look to the brilliance of Adolph Hitler: "It is the press, above all, which wages a positively fanatical and slanderous struggle, tearing down everything which can be regarded as a support of national independence, cultural elevation, and the economic independence of the nation." -Mein Kampf31

In the book "1984", a dystopian fantasy book written by English novelist George Orwell in 1949, Mr. Orwell wrote of a "Ministry of Truth". One of the primary jobs of the Ministry of Truth was to re-write the past to support the current "truth" invented by the party. It was tasked with creating a never-ending string of lies that always prove that the party was right. Now, obviously, we aren't in a strong enough position (yet) to accomplish this as well as the fictitious Ministry of Truth. However, our overwhelming presence in the ranks of educators puts us in a good position to influence our most gullible and important group of all: young people. As new textbooks are released, they are being rewritten in a manner to quietly and effectively introduce the next generations to our version of reality.

This is intentionally done quietly and without fanfare in order to reduce the likelihood of the conservatives fighting back against these changes. "Let me control the textbooks, and I will control the state." ~Adolf Hitler[32] The state of California has taken great strides into the introduction of liberal ideals and viewpoints to children. For example, we were able (with assistance from our incredible liberal warriors, Planned Parenthood and the ACLU), to get legislation passed in California that will force all schools to include our version of sexual education in the state curriculums.

With the brilliantly named California Healthy Youth Act 33, we are now introducing (with detailed descriptions) masturbation, mutual masturbation, fisting, blood play, hook-ups, oral and anal sex, and our version of what gender is. As reported by the California School Choice Foundation, the schools are required by law to teach LGBT friendly views "and teaches kids that their basic identity — as male or female — is something fluid or changeable" [33]

We are taking advantage of the fact that these children are at their most vulnerable and impressionable age to introduce them to our indoctrination and the state government it literally mandating it! Why do I include this in the chapter on lies? As mentioned earlier in the book, we want to disguise our legislative efforts under the flag of public safety or other acceptable ruses to camouflage our actual intent. This law is called the "California Healthy Youth Act" and is presented as a pregnancy and HIV prevention program, but just like our other laws that we promote, it has our actual agenda packed into it.

If we want to be able to jockey ourselves into position to continue our move towards Socialism (and therefore our position of power), the young people of our country need to continue to thing that our ideas are the only correct ideas. " Ideas are more powerful than guns. We would not let our enemies have guns. Why should we let them have ideas?" ~Joseph Stalin34

Their young, idealistic minds must be saturated with our ideas, and only our ideas. Once again, they should be shielded from the truth and infected with the beliefs that our agenda is morally right and beneficial to them. "Keep people from their history, and they are easily controlled." ~Karl Marx35

The takeaway from this chapter is simple. The truth is what you say it is. If we are to achieve our goals, we must be willing to lie, to cheat, to slander. When the truth supports our stance, great, use it. However, if the truth is not useable, no problem, change it. Invent historical events, manipulate statistics, forget obstructive facts, and simply lie, lie, LIE!

Attribute ridiculous statements or claims to Republican politicians. Don't be afraid to make your lies big. And repeat them over and over. Encourage others to repeat them. Push the party agenda! Once you have done this long enough, it will become second nature. If you question the effectiveness of this, just look at our Democratic politicians, they can lie without batting an eye.

Chapter 13

Playing the Long Game

Former president Barrack Obama spoke of "fundamentally transforming the United States of America".36 This is exactly what we are doing. In fact, I would argue that it has already been done. The culture and beliefs of the general population of the country has been systematically altered to better support our eventual take over. The easiest way to see this is to look at popular entertainment. If you take a critical look at the television shows and movies currently being produced, we have our liberal ideas planted in nearly every one. Sometimes it's subtle, but other times we don't even try to hide it.

Make the show interesting. Make it relatable. Get a large following hooked and then just start increasing the amount of liberal propaganda in the material. Most times the audience is so engrossed in the show, they won't even recognize the slow brainwashing being done. Even if they do see it, most will still continue to watch the show because Americans like their TV. They want to sit back and be entertained. This is the perfect media to pour an unending supply of our propaganda directly into their receptive brains.

Hollywood, generally speaking, has been left-leaning for decades. However, this new, overt embracing of leftist ideals is accelerating the push of our agendas. You may have already noticed a change in everything from movies to common TV commercials. Nearly everything will now slip in an LGBT character or scenario. Even children's cartoons are now full of gay characters or even gay parents of a child.

We are sowing the seeds in the young that being gay in America is completely normal, and very common, despite the fact that statistically, it is actually not common. This is being pushed so effectively that most of the minority groups are now over-represented, skewing the children's view of the country. There was even a commercial selling crackers that had a cast of men dressed in drag. Crackers!

They are using Drag Queens to sell crackers! This is advancing much faster than anticipated and the advancement towards the moral destruction of the United States is nearly certain. Let's keep in mind that the primary point of movies, television shows and commercials is all the same; to make money. However, just like the single-issue voters we talked about earlier, these producers are so determined to show how tolerant and progressive they are, that they will force the LGBT agenda into the script, even if it does not improve the plot or even make sense. They are willing accomplices in our plan.

There is an old saying that goes something like this:

Hard times produce hard men
Hard men produce good times
Good times produce soft men
Soft men produce hard times, and the cycle repeats

This has proven generally accurate over the years. We are currently in the last part of that. The current generation is soft. They are not accustomed (for the majority) to hard work. They are entitled. They expect to be given what they "deserve". This chapter addresses the Long Game. This has been a long process getting us to where we are now. This did not happen quickly, and it did not happen without significant effort. However, getting this country into the hard times, full of soft men is important for us to be in the position to strike.

For the most part, when the founding fathers of the United States were establishing the country, they were unable to fathom the strength that we would have to destroy it. However, Benjamin Franklin understood the fragility of the system and one of the weaknesses of the design. "When the people find they can vote themselves money, that will herald the end of our Republic." ~Benjamin Franklin38

Guess what? The people have figured it out. The majority doesn't want to work. They want to be comfortable and entertained. They just want to have their "stuff". That is what we promise. They will willingly vote for people and things that are bad for the country as long as they think it will help them get their "stuff" without having to work for it. We are setting up the United States for an economic hardship. We are intentionally driving up inflation. And just like the wild hogs getting caught in the trap, the uneducated masses are unaware of or apathetic towards the fences being put around them, as long as they still have their entertainment. The USSR kept their population in check for many years with free bread lines and the threat of violence. Americans are being kept in check with "free" money and mindless entertainment in the form of liberal TV, movies, and social media.

Humans are hardwired to try to conserve energy. It's an evolutionary holdover from the time when our ancestors didn't know when they would get their next meal. It was important to conserve calories when every bite had to be killed or gathered from the earth. Today, that mindset of conserving your energy translates into a natural tendency for laziness. Many people don't want to work. And why should they? We currently have programs in place that will pay them more to sit at home than to go to work. They can't afford to get a job, because they'll take the pay cut! It's our very own version of the USSR bread lines.

Right now, you may be asking yourself "Why?" Why would we be encouraging giving money away? Why do we discourage people from working? Why are we trying to increase government dependency? Let's look to Sun Tzu, the author of "The Art of War", for the answer to those questions: "An evil enemy will burn his own country to the ground, to rule over the ashes." -Sun Tzu.41 We are trying to foster the slow economic collapse of the United States in order to jockey ourselves into position to rule over the remains.

We are at war here. The conservatives, Christians, Republicans, Constitutionalists, Teabaggers, and all the other right-wingers should be viewed as nothing more than enemies of our long-term goals. The liberals who have gone before us in the previous generations made sacrifices for the big picture. Many of them never saw the fruits of their labor. They never got to enjoy the wealth and power that we enjoy today. However, we are now, finally, in the position to finish the move.

The United States has lost credibility on the world stage. The president is viewed as a weak, bumbling, mumbling dementia-ridden joke. The dollar is being devalued at an astonishing rate. Our military is being shackled by our own federal government. Most importantly, the general population of the United States is finally accepting our view as the reality. It has taken multiple steps over many generations, but victory is now in view.

The collapse of the United States is now just a matter of time. And when it does fail, we, the Liberal Elite will be there to rule over the ashes. We will be prepared to present our plan and call it salvation. We will enslave in the name of security. We will tax and steal in the name of the public good. We will rule as royalty and call it governance.

The End...or at least the beginning of the end...

Author's Note

This book has been a labor of love. I attempted to write it in a manner that would seem just like a conversation with a radical leftist, but I found many parts of it especially hard to write. I found it difficult, even writing sarcastically, to advocate for hurting children, or hating cops. However, I felt that it needed to be said. I felt the need to put it down in writing and say out loud the evil, destructive things that I see happening in the world around me.

I had a friend ask me if I was concerned that the liberals would actually use the book for ideas and therefore by writing it, I would be making the situation worse. I've thought about that question for a long time. Here is my answer: They are already doing the things that I'm describing. By putting them down on paper, by broadcasting them to the target audience, I just hope to make people more aware of it and hopefully provide people a few more tools to defend themselves with. Even with all of our problems, we still have the best chance of any country on earth of maintaining freedom. Don't give up the fight.

Citations

1. https://www.azquotes.com/quote/58378
2. https://www.azquotes.com/quote/816961
3. https://www.azquotes.com/quote/577834
4. https://www.inspiringquotes.us/author/9320-joseph-goebbels/about-propaganda
5. https://wake-up.org/wp-content/uploads/2018/02/Gallup_Poll.pdf
6. https://notamonsterblog.wordpress.com/2017/04/07/7-reasons-why-pedophilia-is-a-sexual-orientation/
7. https://www.azquotes.com/author/5626-Joseph_Goebbels,
8. https://www.nbcnews.com/politics/2020-election/biden-says-poor-kids-are-just-bright-just-talented-white-n1040686
9. https://edition.cnn.com/2020/05/22/politics/biden-charlamagne-tha-god-you-aint-black/index.html
10. https://www.presidency.ucsb.edu/documents/address-before-joint-session-the-congress-the-state-the-union-11

11. https://heavy.com/news/2017/08/maria-chappelle-nadal-missouri-husband-age-facebook-twitter-who-is/
12. https://www.azquotes.com/quote/551234
13. http://www.gospelweb.net/PatrioticWorks/moralorpatrioticquotes.htm
14. https://www.azquotes.com/quote/1255417
15. https://propagandaprinciples.wordpress.com/joseph-goebbels/
16. https://havanatimes.org/opinion/freedom-of-the-press-in-cuba/
17. https://catholicfundamentalism.com/think-press-great-keyboard-government-can-play-joseph-goebbels/9432
18. http://www.muslimtents.com/aminahsworld/Fastest_growing.html
19. https://www.healthyplace.com/gender/glbt-mental-health/homosexuality-and-suicide-lgbt-suicide-a-serious-issue
20. https://www.cnbc.com/video/2018/08/09/drag-kid-desmond-is-amazing-tells-lgbtq-youth-to-be-themselves.html
21. https://americanmilitarynews.com/2021/06/biden-says-gun-owners-would-need-f-15s-and-nukes-to-take-on-the-us-govt/

22. https://www.fox32chicago.com/news/biden-oddly-suggests-150-million-people-killed-by-guns-since-2007

23. https://www.lexico.com/en/definition/terrorism

24. https://seekingalpha.com/instablog/25783813-peter-palms/4595906-terrorism-is-best-political-weapon-for-nothing-drives-people-harder-fear-of-sudden-death

25. https://jsaulburton.com/2017/05/15/it-is-not-truth-which-matters-but-victory/

26. https://hungarianspectrum.org/2016/03/03/adolf-hitler-if-you-tell-a-big-enough-lie-and-tell-it-frequently-enough-it-will-be-believed/

27. https://www.inspiringquotes.us/author/9320-joseph-goebbels/about-lying

28. https://www.usnews.com/news/blogs/press-past/2013/01/25/bill-clinton-15-years-ago-i-did-not-have-sexual-relations-with-that-woman

29. https://www.politifact.com/obama-like-health-care-keep/

30. http://libertytree.ca/quotes/Bill.Clinton.Quote.6647

31. Hitler, Adolf, 1889-1945. *Mein Kampf*. Boston: Houghton Mifflin, 1999.

32. https://www.azquotes.com/quote/566434

33. https://www.californiaschoolchoice.org/what_you_should_know_about_california_sex_education

34. https://www.stridentconservative.com/erase-history-and-you-control-the-people/

35. https://www.azquotes.com/author/9564-Karl_Marx

36. https://www.dailymotion.com/video/x6e32iu

37. https://www.facebook.com/watch/?v=1386309134771731

38. http://libertytree.ca/quotes/Benjamin.Franklin.Quote.CC66

39. https://www.bbc.com/news/world-us-canada-57387350

40. https://inspirationfeed.com/sun-tzu-quotes/

41. https://www.reddit.com/r/quotes/comments/kvihf5/an_evil_enemy_will_burn_his_own_nation_to_the/

Connect with Blacksmith Publishing

www.thepinelander.com

Books by Blacksmith Publishing

Small Unit Tactics Handbook

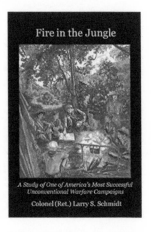

Fire in the Jungle

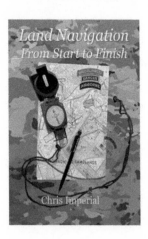

Land Navigation From Start to Finish

Tactical Leadership

Books by Blacksmith Publishing

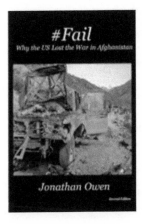

Fail

Confederate Black Ops

Active Shooter Awareness and Response

Marriage is a Four-Letter Word

Books by Blacksmith Publishing

God's Man

Iron Sharpening Iron

Unto the Thousandth Generation

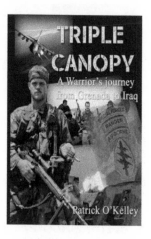

Triple Canopy

Books by Blacksmith Publishing

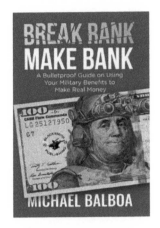

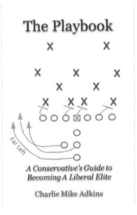

Break Rank Make Bank

The Playbook

www.blacksmithpublishingcom

Lightning Source UK Ltd.
Milton Keynes UK
UKHW040836030122
396544UK00003B/258